AF226124

A PAPER-CUT CHRISTMAS
Legends of the Gift Giver

A PAPER-CUT CHRISTMAS
Legends of the Gift Giver

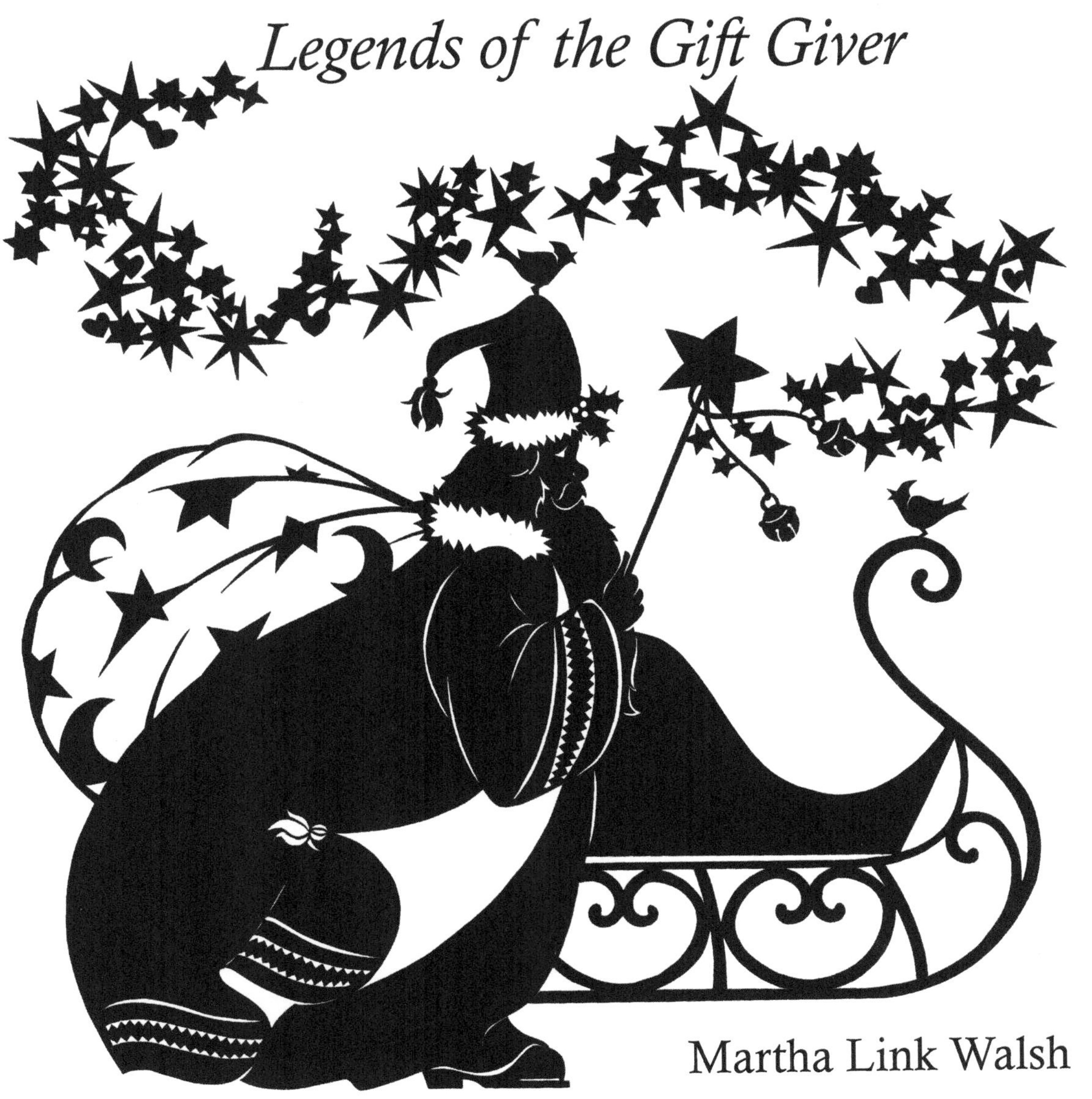

Martha Link Walsh

To my Mom
who is always beside me
but never more than at Christmastime

CONTENTS

ACKNOWLEDGEMENTS   ix

INTRODUCTION   xi

Nature's Santa   2

The Peaceable Kingdom   4

Mother and Son   6

The Three Kings   8

Holland's Sinterklaas   10

Saint Nicholas, Patron Saint of Children   12

Saint Nicholas, Patron Saint of Sailors   14

The Christmas Rose   16

Bavaria's Christkindl   18

Germany's Weihnachtsmann   20

Hungary's Mikulas and Jezuska   22

Sweden's Santa Lucia   24

Czechoslovakia's Svaty Mikulas and Jezisek   26

Russia's Ded Moroz   28

Poland's Swiety Mikolaj and Gwiazdor   30

Ireland's Daidi na Hollag   32

France's Pere Noel   34

Denmark's Nisse   36

Italy's Lady Befana   38

Finland's Joulupukki   40

England's Father Christmas   42

America's Santa Claus   44

The Christmas Tree   46

The Christmas Wreath   48

BIBLIOGRAPHY   51

Acknowledgements

My heartfelt thanks go to:

…generations of families around the world, whose legends and traditions have faithfully kept the spirit of Christmas alive through many centuries. Their obvious joy and faith have inspired my artwork.

…my family, whose support and encouragement in paper-cutting has sustained me for over 40 years. My mother's insight and love introduced me to my life's work and to the magic of Christmas. My sister, Mary, has forever been my Doberman and my Santa Claus. Her unconditional love and protective spirit are my constant companions. My Dad's attention to detail and design, together with his enthusiastic encouragement and pride in my work, has been my rock. My husband, Fran, is ever-present in his unselfish sacrifices to see me find satisfaction and success in my work.

…my loyal customers, whose unflagging support enables me to continue my art, and whose enthusiasm and praise is highly motivating from day to day. I am proud of how much they have come to appreciate the art form of paper-cutting, too.

…Margie Sigman, friend and editor, who generously gave me her expertise with humor, kindness and understanding.

…Jen Payne, cheerleader, friend, and promoter, who has kept me on track to fulfill a dream. Her knowledgeable nudges have encouraged, guided, and helped me in my work and in this book.

…K&G Graphics, printers extraordinaire, who have assisted me in every step of my career with generosity, humor and expertise.

Every story in this book is a testament to love and kindnesses shown. I have been very fortunate to be blessed with all of that. I am forever grateful.

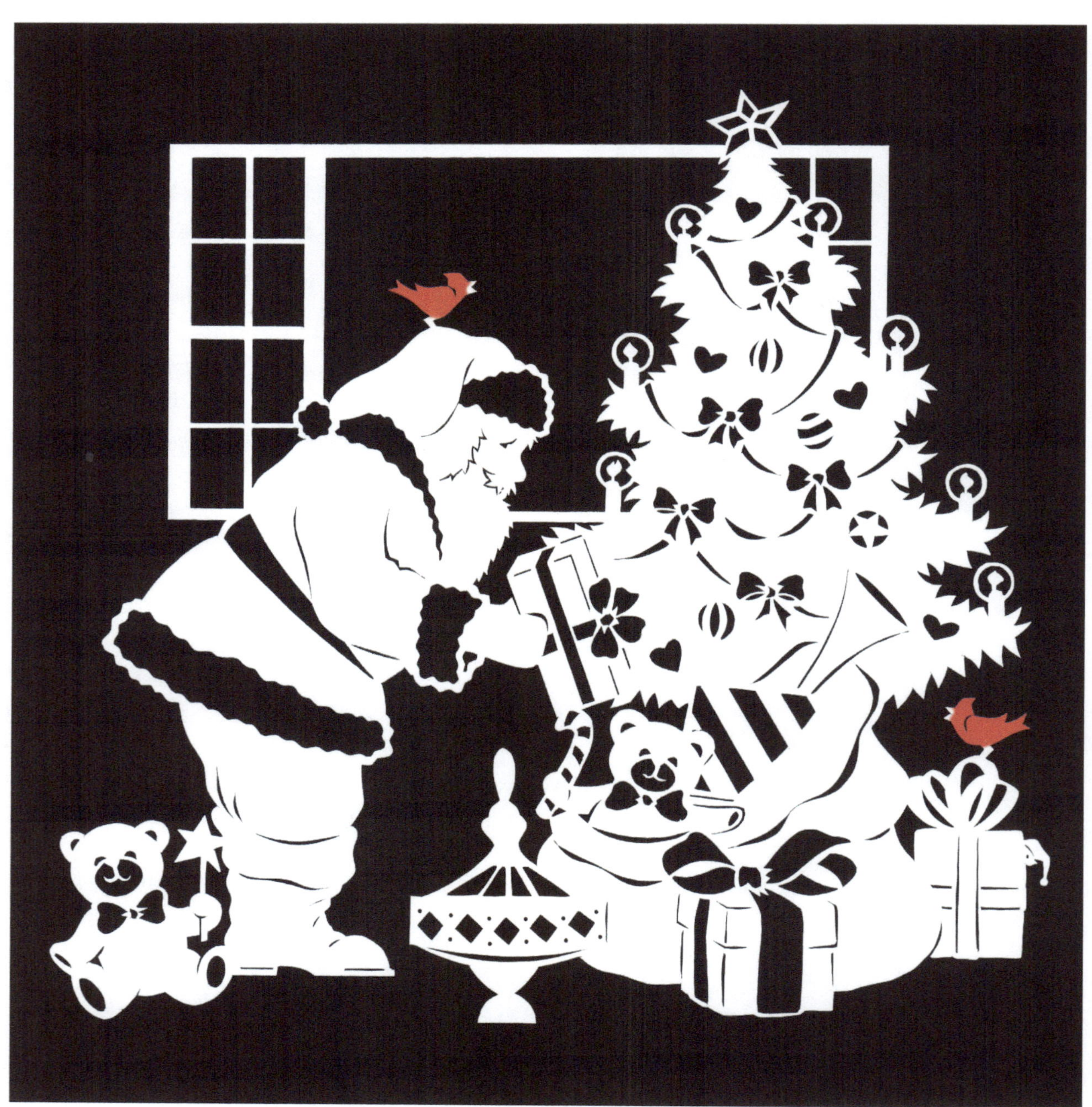

Introduction

Christmas has forever been a treasured holiday for me, in large part because my parents tried hard to create lasting family rituals and traditions for their three children. They had magical ways of making something beautiful out of the simplest things, and they encouraged us to do the same. One of my favorite memories was the year when the wall separating the living room from the kitchen was still unfinished. Mom made our home into a literal pine forest by weaving fir boughs in and around the open studs. The sight and scent was transporting.

Our Christmas tree was another creative masterpiece. Tiny white lights and a hint of tinsel illuminated the hundreds of small trinkets-turned-ornaments from Mom and Dad's travels over the years. Handmade bead-and-glass ornaments, some of them made in Hungary and handed down through many generations, completed the fantasy, right there in our living room. Add Mom's Hungarian nut-roll, Gram's fruitcake, and Aunt Millie's date-filled oatmeal cookies, and we had a feast for all our senses.

Paper-cutting

When I was recuperating from a long illness, Mom gave me her embroidery scissors and paper to pass idle time. I whiled away many hours "playing" with cutting paper, not realizing it could be anything serious. Little did we know that it would become my life's passion and career! Once again, tradition and "made-by-hand" had captured my imagination.

The art of paper-cutting is a time-honored practice around the world. After the Chinese invented paper during the first century A.D., folk artists (and now fine artists) began cutting images to ward away evil spirits, decorate gifts, illustrate stories, or adorn their walls. From Mexico to Germany to Japan, artists have expressed feelings, ideas, and stories in their cut-paper art. Like all art forms, cut-paper artistry is a study in lore and legends, revealing much about cultures, beliefs, and even politics.

Creating the Paper-Cut Images

The process of cutting the images begins with a rough sketch to play with different sizes, placement, and shapes of key elements I hope to include in a design. This sketch may be done many, many times, but often the initial image I have in my mind's eye is what is ultimately most pleasing (and workable).

That sketch is then further refined with attention to the positive and negative spaces, to the connections among the elements, the proportions of each one, and the overall balance and weight of the design. Once the drawing is finalized, it is transferred to the acid-free paper and redrawn, ready to cut.

Then the fun starts! Using surgical scissors and scalpels, I first cut the negative spaces from the center to the perimeter, watching the images emerge, like magic! The rest is then cut, always from the center to the outside, being careful that all the elements stay connected so it remains a single piece of paper.

Once cut, it is mounted onto acid-free matting. Using very small dabs of glue, I adhere only select parts of the cutting to the matting. This allows much of the image to lift, giving subtle shadows and dimension to the overall artwork.

Gift-Giver Legends

As my paper-cutting evolved from a pastime to a full-time obsession, the magic of the Christmas season seemed like the perfect time to showcase the magic of the art form. The legend of the gift-giver became my focus. Where did gift-giving start? Why do people do it? What does it say about a culture? Each fall I began immersing myself in the myths and traditions of gift-givers. Again and again, I encountered the gift-giver character whose goodness remained the same but whose name changed among cultures, from Odin and Saint Nicholas to Father Frost and Santa Claus.

Each year, I would chose one country or a part of the Christmas story to illustrate with a paper-cutting. Connecting a very old art form with even older stories gave me a great sense of continuity. Plus, I was afraid that the Coca-Cola Santa Claus, invented so recently (mid 20th century), was edging out those fine old gift-giving fellows in people's hearts and minds. I made it my job to keep them, and their rich stories, alive.

So here I am, 40 years later…witnessing the wonder and joy on my customers' faces when they discover an authentic gift-giver story from their family's place of origin. Italy's Lady Befana, Russia's Grandfather Frost, and Finland's Joulupukki are just a few of the legends collected and illustrated here.

Symbols of the Season

This end-of-the-year holiday is the perfect time to count our blessings, to pause to acknowledge our past, and to enjoy a sort of "time out"—a few moments with our inner child. The two cardinals in each of the images are included to give continuity to the gift-giver evolution. They represent, for me, the beauty and energy of nature, even in the dead of winter.

They serve, too, as witness to a friendship that will be with me forever. Marilyn Rosenquist shared my passion for this winter holiday and was the inspiration for the gift-giver series. Her "ho-ho room" was her own Santa's workshop for months. The red cardinals represent her friendship, her love of color, her generosity of spirit, and her pure joy throughout the holiday.

My hope is that in our fast-paced time, this book will help you feel the same sense of wonder that I do at Christmas. I hope to bring you new stories, new joy, and new springboards for your imagination during the season of giving.

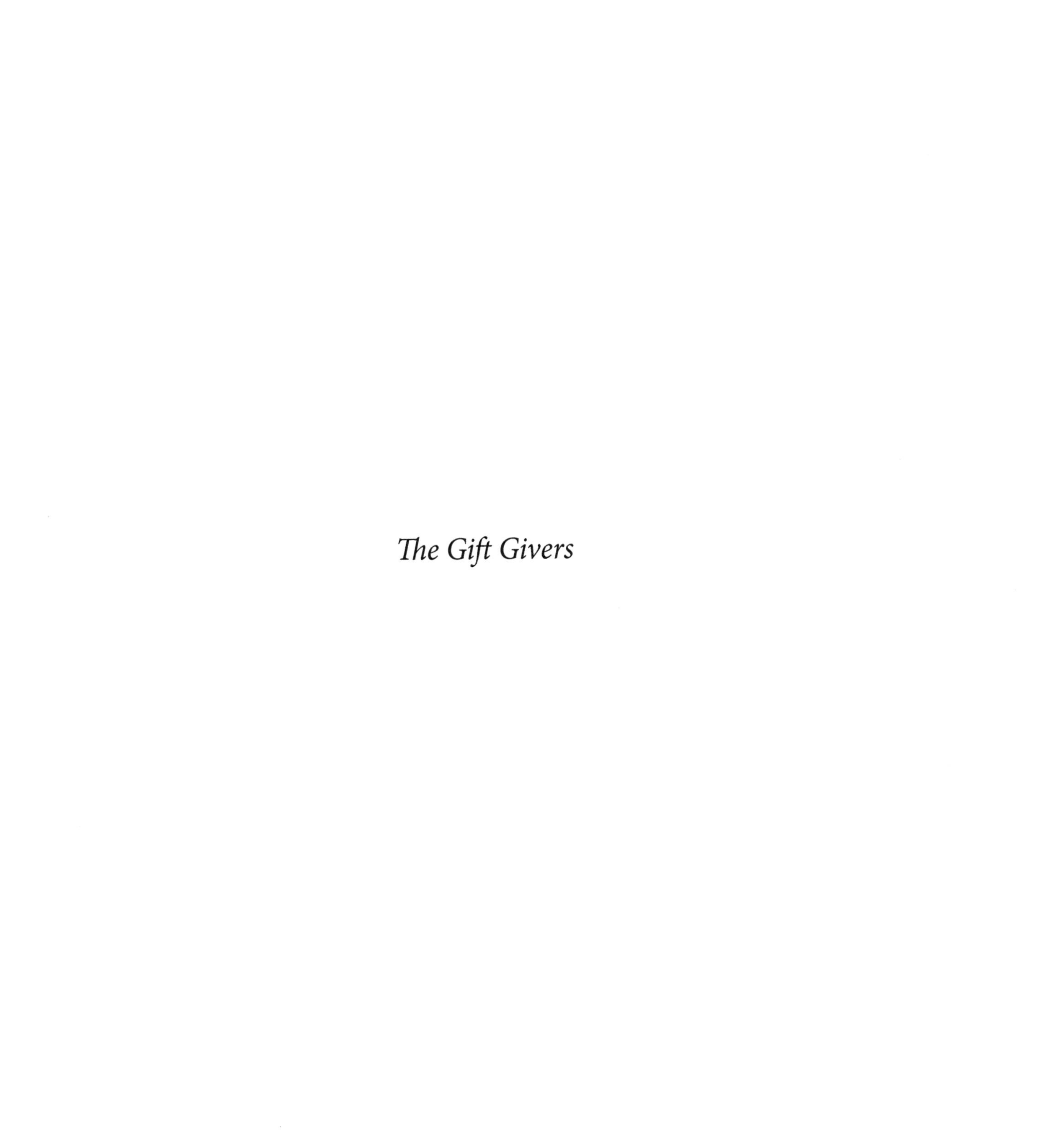

The Gift Givers

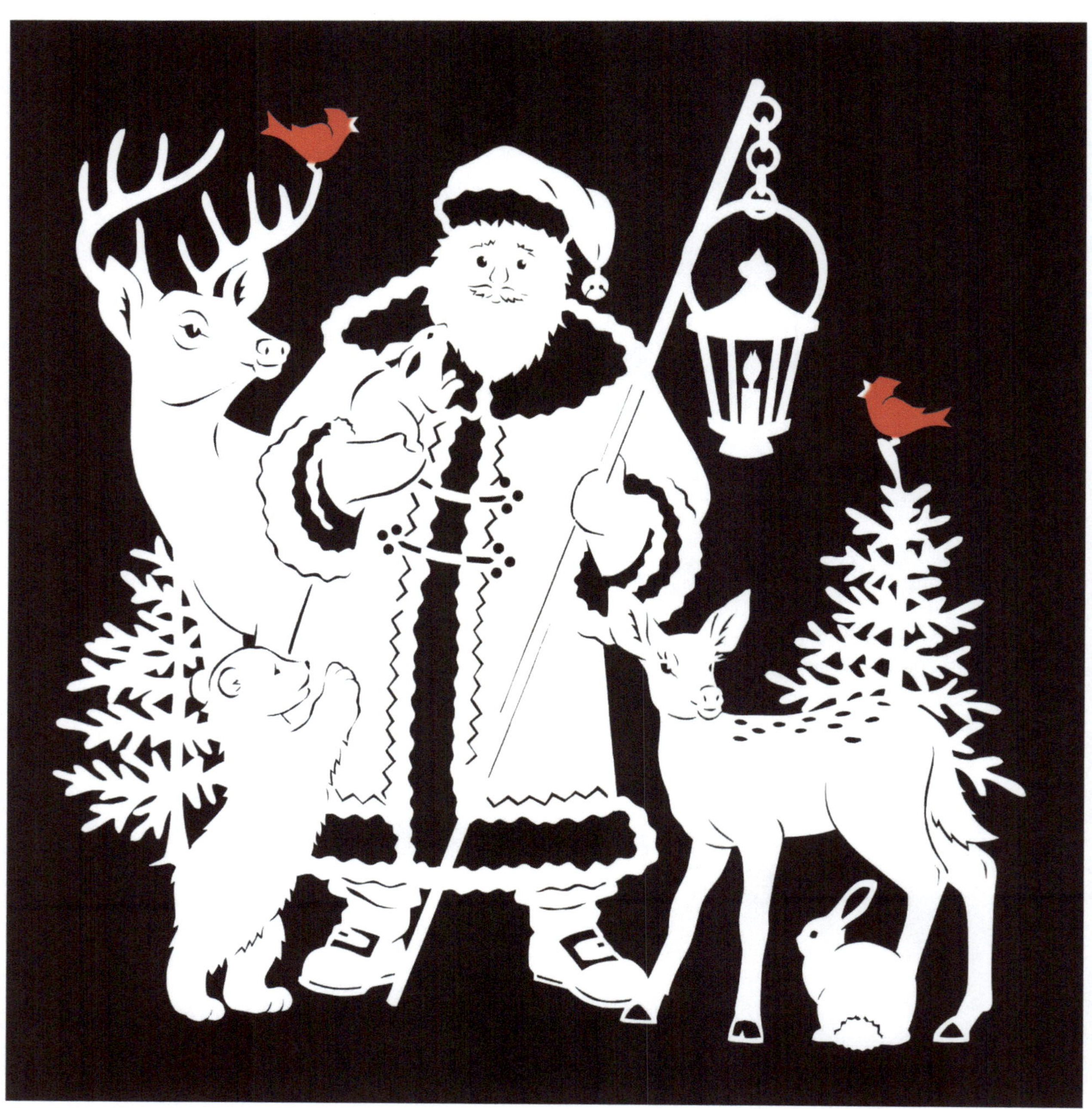

Nature's Santa

From earliest times the lore of gods and goddesses explained the unknown or inexplicable to pagan civilizations and created a sort of order in their lives. Natural phenomena like lightning or thunder, or the virtues and strengths of particular plants and animals, were assigned a deity that explained their presence. Over time, different cultures created elaborate traditions in hopes of pleasing those entities and ensuring safety or a new season of prosperity.

The end of the seasonal calendar year was always a celebratory time. Before Christianity found its way to ancient Rome, the winter solstice, or Festival of Lights, was a time of revelry to honor Saturn, the harvest god, and Mithras, the god of light. People exchanged ritualistic gifts to express hope and goodwill. Twigs of laurel and evergreen, for instance, symbolized rebirth and new life; candles symbolized warmth and the return of the sun. Simple pastries and sweets promised a bountiful year. Such celebrations surely boosted morale and welcomed the coming year with hope.

The early church called these cheerful celebrations an abomination. Church leaders felt strongly that winter traditions should be solemn and marked by religious devotion. However, they also knew that absorbing some of the old rituals so near and dear to the hearts of the people would aid in their conversion to Christianity. So the leaders compromised. They allowed the ancient tradition of giving gifts to continue, in the guise of the wise men giving gifts to the Baby Jesus, and they allowed people to celebrate through the ceremony of the Christian Mass.

In this peaceful scene, animals from time immemorial gather with a generic Santa figure who carries a lantern to light the way. Just as the animals give gifts to the Christ Child, the gift-giver brings them the gifts of light, peace, and goodwill.

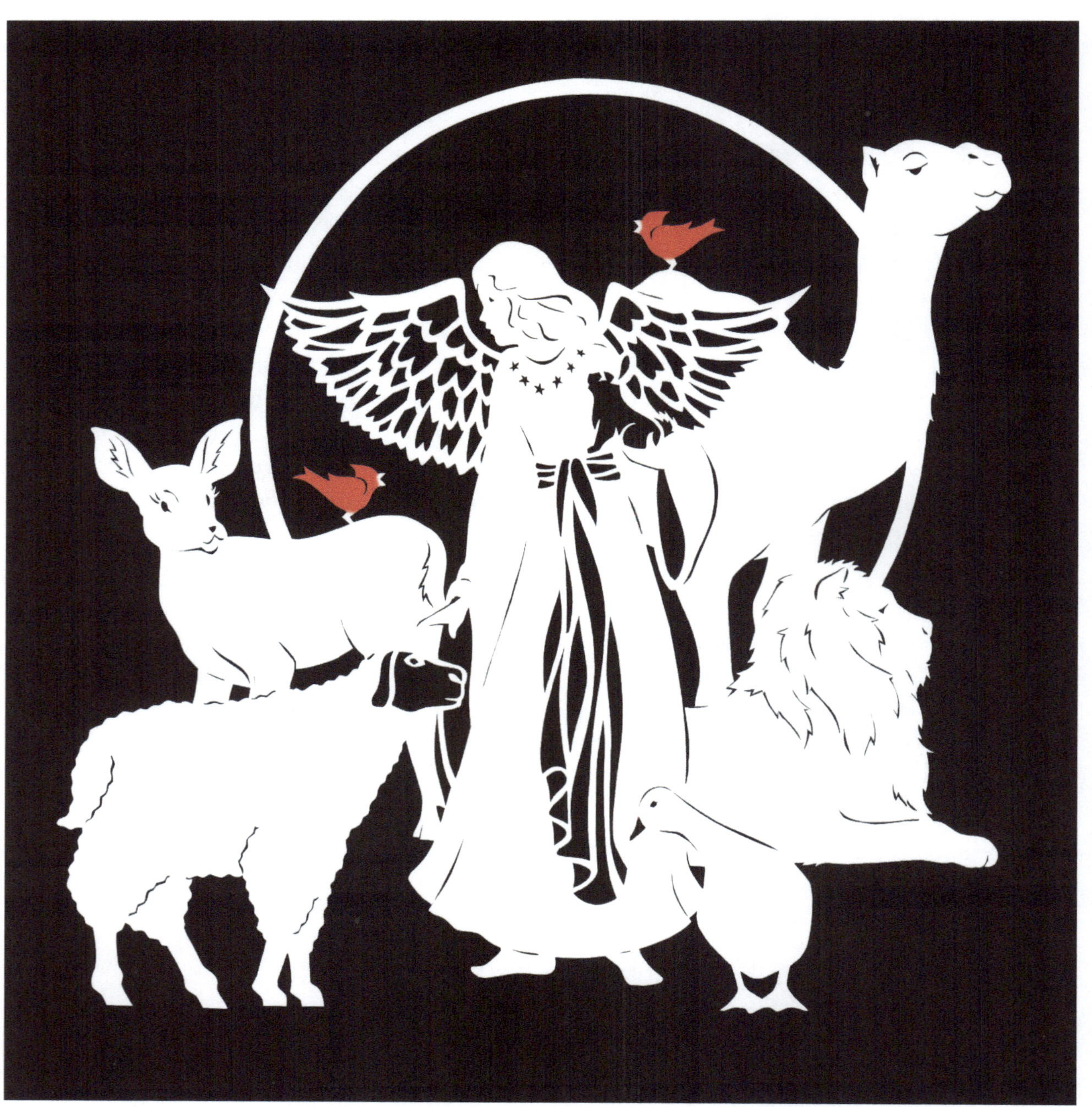

The Peaceable Kingdom

Over centuries of recounting the miracle of Jesus' birth, storytellers began to include animals in the tale, giving each of them a role to play. The steadfast donkey carried Mary to the stable in Bethlehem, the gentle cow gave up her manger for His bed, the wooly sheep warmed Him with her soft coat, the doves cooed Him to sleep, and so on. The underlying messages of generosity of spirit, purity of heart, and selfless kindness add to the benevolence of the scene.

Some accounts say that God gifted the animals with speech on that night, as a way of saying thanks for their gifts to His Son. So, at midnight on every Christmas Eve, imagine all animals talking aloud and sharing their memories of the past year or their hopes for the one coming.

Christian teachings have added yet another dimension to the manger scene by associating each animal with a desirable personality trait. Thus, the steadfast donkey is now seen as a devoted and loyal follower. The lamb is a symbol of devotion to God. The animal's innocence is a gentle metaphor about the benefits of living a just and peaceable life on earth. Once again the animals have created a means of support, philosophically and emotionally.

Christmas is about giving thanks, and the selfless giving of the animals present on Christmas night is a powerful symbol of that. Just as animals protect and nurture their young, so do old and new belief systems nurture us. In this design, a guardian angel or goddess of love stands with the animals of the field and forest, gathered together in peace and goodwill.

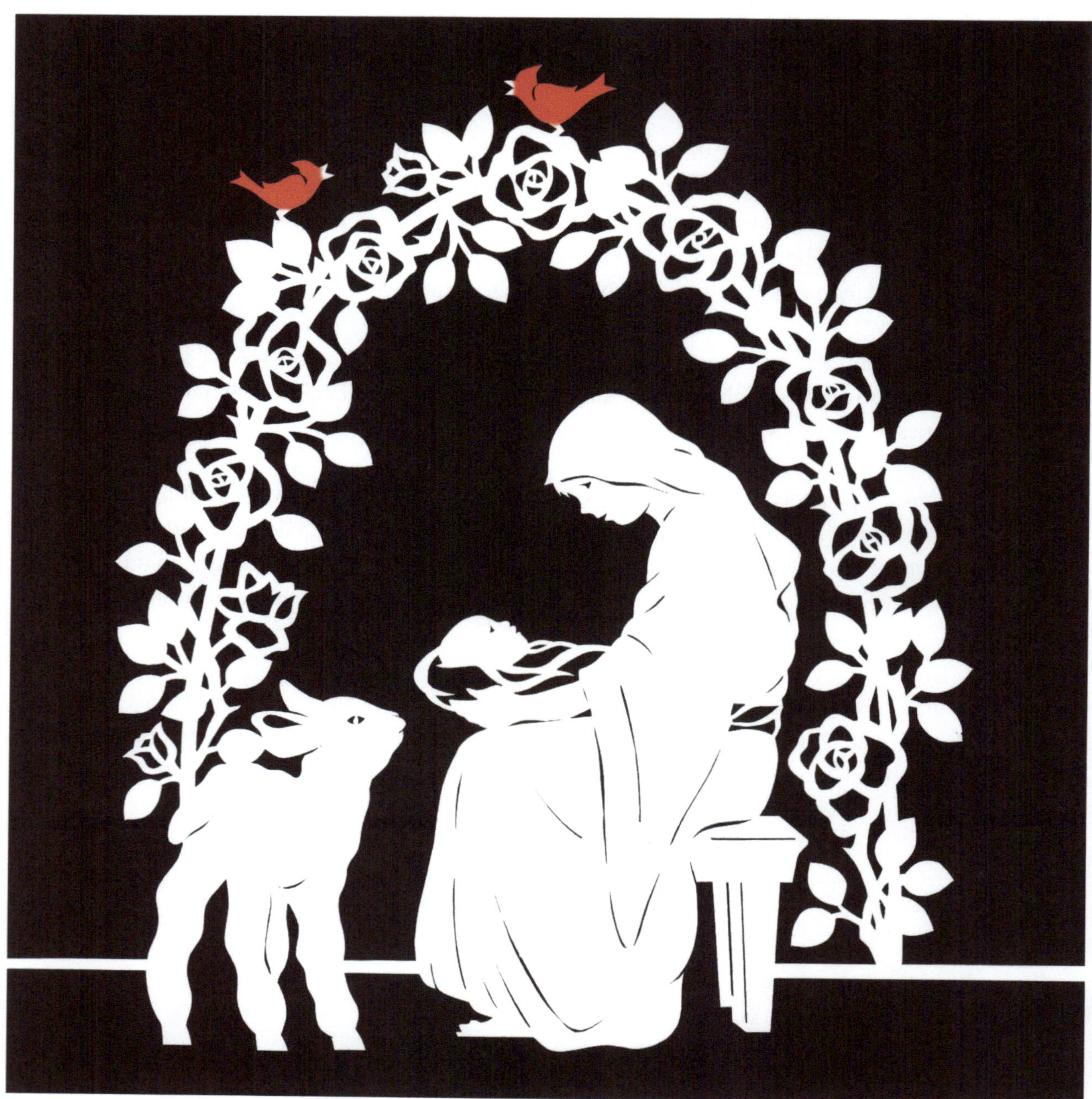

Mother and Son

Mary and her newborn child are the essence of Christmas. The story of the nativity has been told in thousands of artworks, in oral storytellings worldwide, in plays, music, and songs. Children use a nativity crèche and figurines to tell and retell the story as they get ready for Christmas Eve. The nativity also teaches Christian beliefs and values through symbols and story.

During the Middle Ages, Christians thought of the rose as the queen of all flowers, and so made it the symbol for the Virgin Mary and other holy women. Long before that time, the Romans had associated the rose with Venus, their goddess of beauty, just as the Greeks chose the rose for their goddess of love, Aphrodite. To Victorians, who gave many flowers a special meaning or message, the rose represented love and friendship. They believed that the passionate color of the red rose could symbolize a giving of one's self to greater purposes. The white rose came to stand for purity, innocence, and faith.

While the arch has long been an important building tool, its curving shape also suggests protection and safety. Artists use the image to show or imply a safe path or passageway. Taking that idea of physical safety a little further, the arch can suggest emotional safety, too. As Christianity sought to distance people from their old pagan beliefs, archways in paintings, churches, and public places came to symbolize moving forward toward a safe place that offered sanctuary.

In ancient times, the lamb was a symbol of both wealth and sacrifice. Early people depended on healthy lambs to expand their flock, increase their social standing, and provide wool, leather, and milk. It was appropriate, then, for sheep to come with the shepherds to be witnesses at the nativity. Later Christian teachings used the lamb as a symbol of Jesus and also of his faithful and trusting followers.

In this image, the Virgin Mary, protected by an archway of white roses, cradles her Son as a gentle lamb looks on. The symbols communicate love, protection, innocence, purity, faith, peace.

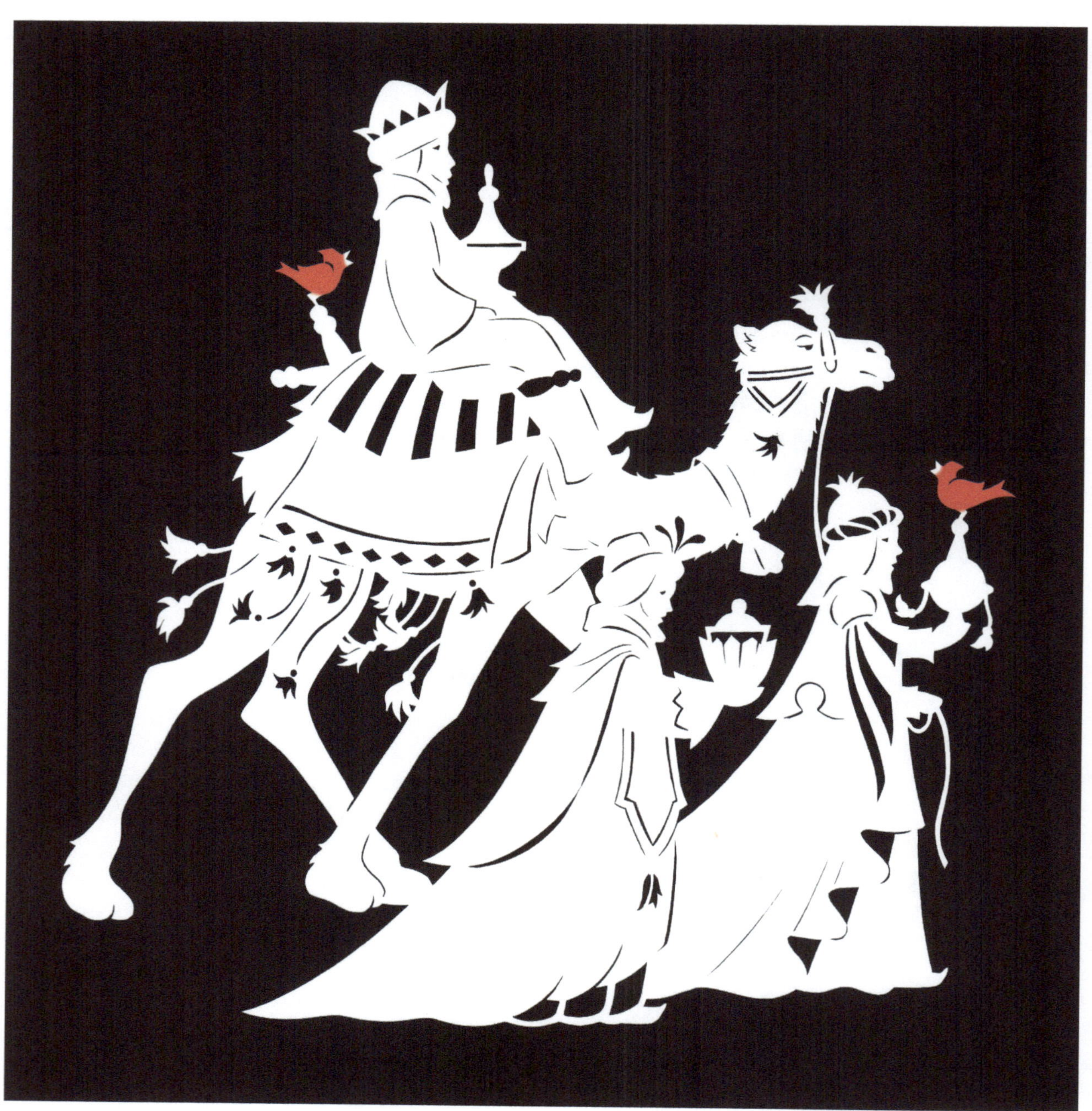

The Three Kings

One of the earliest instances of gift-giving in Christian teachings was of course the journey to Bethlehem by the three magi, or kings. Born into wealth, all three were well educated and of considerable influence. It is said that each of them had independently been studying the stars, noting changes and patterns. On the day of Jesus's birth, a bright new star appeared in the heavens. Astrologers had been watching for it, because the prophet Balaam had predicted that the appearance of a new star meant a savior had arrived. Each of these adventurous scholars decided to travel to Bethlehem to give witness to Him. This star acted as a faithful guide for Melchior of Persia, Gaspar of Tarsus, and Balthazar of Saba. When the magi met along the way, and realized they had a common goal, they set out together for the rest of the journey. Each man was grateful for the company and also anxious to find the Christ Child. They had all put great thought into their gifts and wanted to deliver them safely to Him.

Melchior's gift was an apple of gold and gilt coins, which helped finance the Holy Family's flight into Egypt. Gold represented purity, divinity and immortality and symbolized that Jesus was an earthly king. Gaspar brought myrrh, a resin used as incense and medication that was believed to strengthen children. The dark red crystals symbolized mortality, suffering, and healing, and testified that the baby was an earthly man. Balthazar's urn of frankincense, a resin of the boswellia tree, represented prayer and sacrifice. Believing the baby was a god, his gift spoke to His future.

Today, on the Eve of Epiphany (January sixth), the children of Spain believe that the magi travel through Spain on their annual pilgrimage to Bethlehem. Knowing them as the famous gift-givers, children leave their empty shoes out on the windowsill, alongside a plate of food for the travelers and hay for their camels, in hopes of waking to presents left in the night.

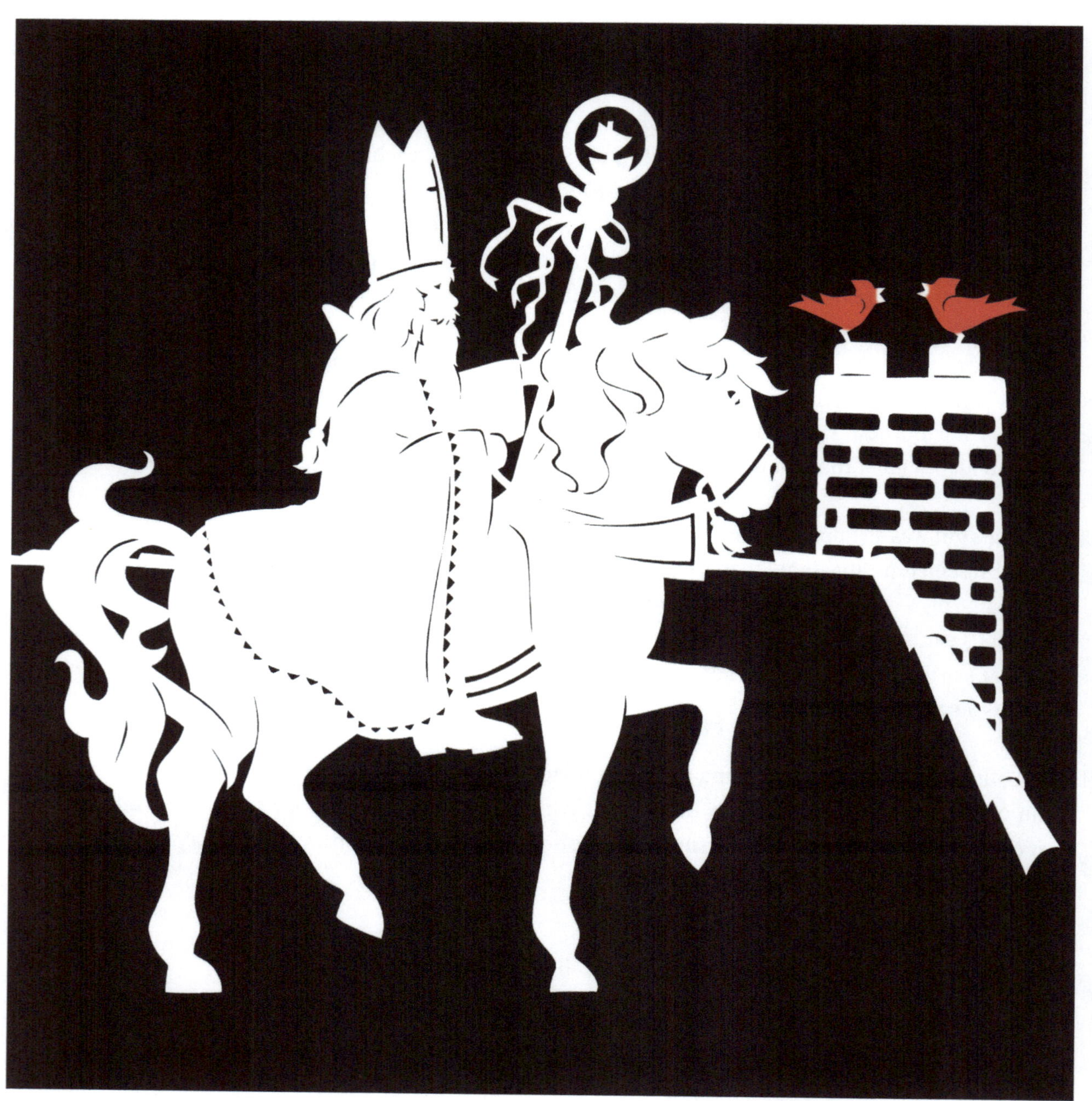

Holland's Sinterklaas

One of the first legends of a gift-giving folk hero came from the pagan myth of Odin, the northern European god of wisdom and magic. He was depicted as a tall, white-bearded old man who rode across the skies on his eight-legged white horse. It was believed that if you revered him, he would continue to protect you and, to show his thanks, would reward you with presents. That belief spawned the tradition of children leaving treats for him, and hay and carrots for his horse on their hearth or doorstep. In return, they hoped to see gifts from Odin the next morning.

A new legend replaced Odin in the fourth century with the spread of Christianity. Nicholas, the Byzantine bishop from Myra (Turkey), was renowned for his loving kindness and generosity, his many miracles, and his habit of taking presents to the needy. The church elevated him from local hero to saint, and the tradition of giving surprise gifts to reward good behavior was continued.

Unfortunately, the Reformation of the 16th and 17th centuries forbade the veneration of saints in Europe. The Dutch, however, refused to comply, and created Sinterklaas. Combining aspects of both Odin and Nicholas, the new gift-giver was a kind and wise old bishop who rode a white horse named Amerigo (now with only four legs).

Sinterklaas is said to arrive in mid-November from Spain on a ship laden with gifts. He rides through the night, lands on the roofs, and listens through the chimneys to be sure that good children live there. Some people think he delivers gifts at night; others insist he comes during the day, leaving gifts by the front door. Either way, he and his surprises are anxiously awaited.

A modern addition in Holland is Christmas Man. Like Santa Claus, he arrives from the north (Lapland) on Christmas Eve to deliver gifts. Christmas Man is now part of the Christmas tradition, but Sinterklaas is still the gift-giver near and dear to the hearts of the Dutch.

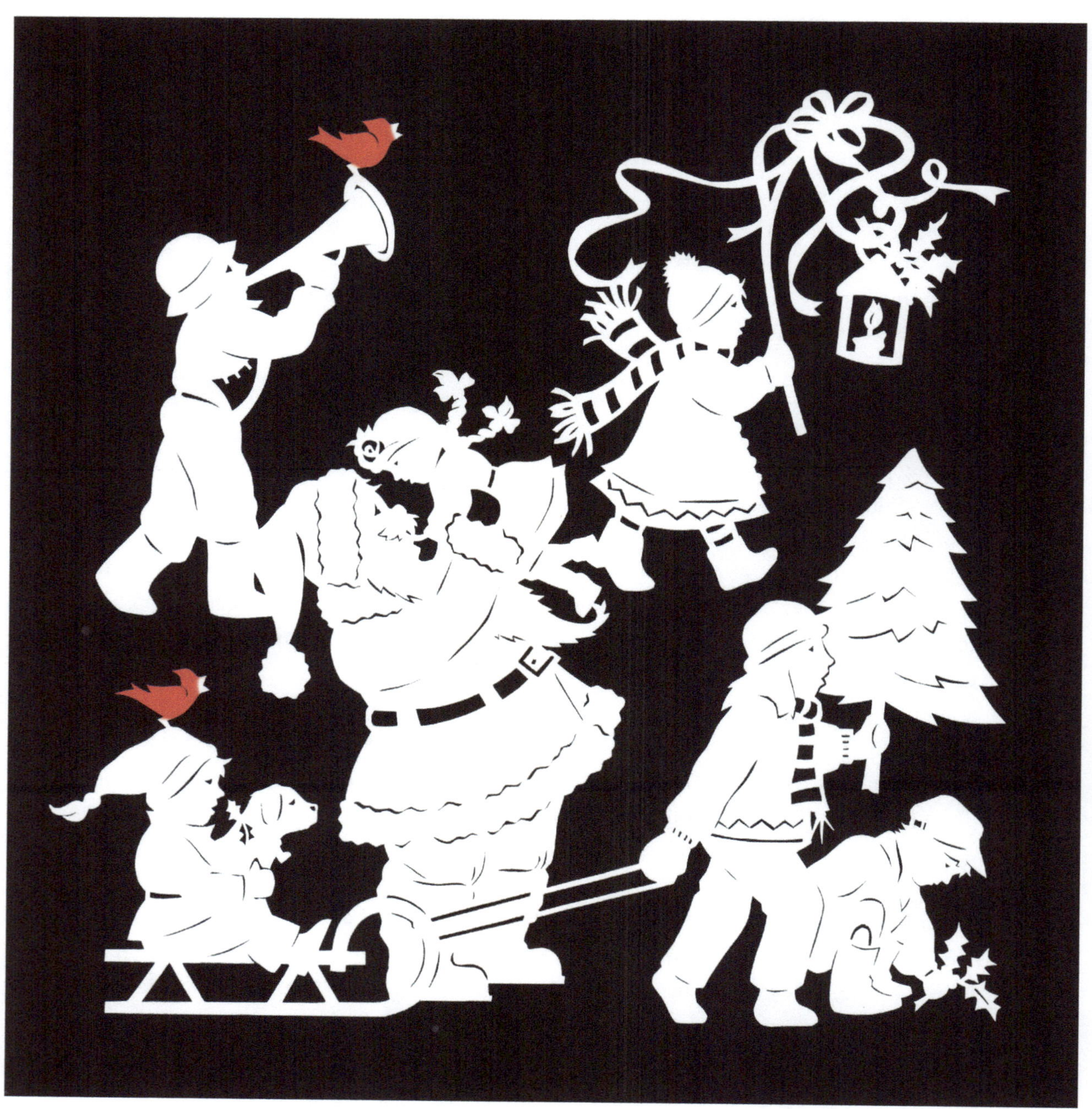

Saint Nicholas, Patron Saint of Children

Bishop Nicholas, even as a young man, was known for his secret generosity toward those in need, particularly disadvantaged children. His sainthood is based on the many stories of selfless, courageous deeds on behalf of others.

One legend tells of three unmarried girls from Patras, Greece. Sadly, the family had no money to offer as dowries to prospective husbands. Lacking funds to support his daughters, their father feared they might have to be sold into a dubious occupation. Mysteriously, on three occasions a bag of gold found its way into the home during the night, saving the sisters. When the last gift was tossed through the open window (landing in a stocking hung by the fire to dry), the girls' father spied the gift-giver—Bishop Nicholas.

As other stories of the bishop's secret kindnesses spread, anyone receiving unexpected anonymous gifts attributed them to the good man. One tale tells of him bringing back to life three boys who had been robbed for their money and killed by a wicked innkeeper. After having seen the crime in a dream, St. Nicholas went to the tavern, found the culprit, and saved the boys.

After Nicholas's death, the townspeople of Myra, Turkey, erected a church in his name. A legend tells that once, during services honoring Nicholas, a band of pirates came into the city and looted the church. Not satisfied with only gold, gem-encrusted treasures, and a golden chalice, the robbers snatched a young boy, Basilios, to become their emir's personal cupbearer.

A year later, his mother was at home saying a silent prayer for her son's safe return. At that same moment, Basilios was serving his foreign master a drink in the golden chalice. The story says that Saint Nicholas appeared before him, blessed him, and miraculously transported him home to his mother, still holding the chalice. Incredibly, Saint Nicholas had answered her prayers.

It is no surprise that this generous bishop and patron saint became so prominent in Christmas gift-giving traditions. The myths we cherish about Saint Nicholas, the anticipation we enjoy on Christmas morning, and the love we show in our family traditions during the holidays, all honor this righteous man.

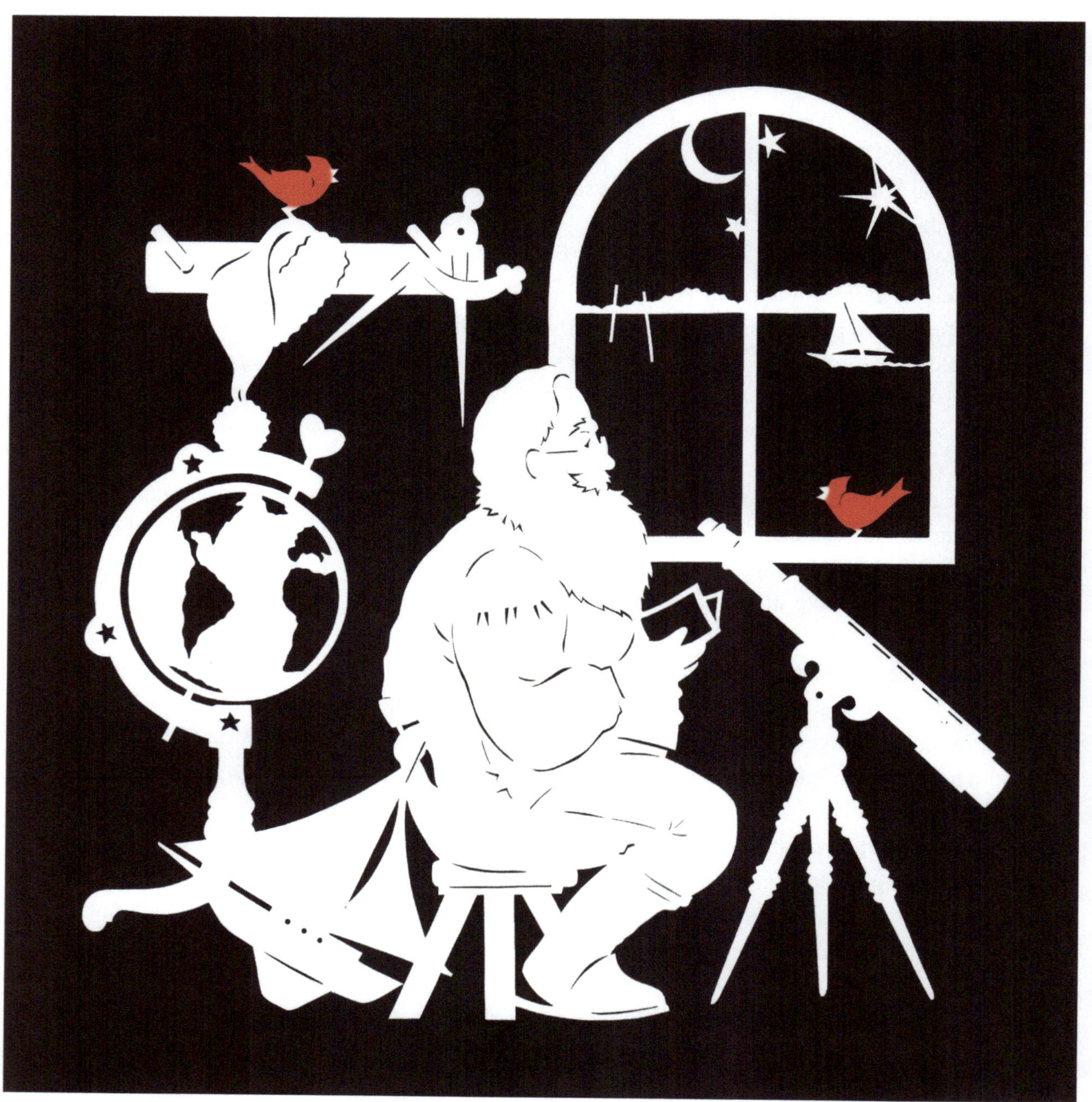

Saint Nicholas, Patron Saint of Sailors

Imagine you are living centuries ago in Turkey or Greece. You are on what feels like a tiny boat in a very large sea. It is cold, and howling winds send treacherous waves crashing onto the ship's deck. You have heard stories about the "Christianized Poseidon," Saint Nicholas, who has saved a multitude of sailors from perishing at sea. So, in desperation, you pray to him for help.

Suddenly, a vision appears—someone grabs the tiller, steadies the deck, and calms the sea. You are safe, but when you look again, the vision is gone. Once safely on land, you run to church to give thanks for your miraculous rescue. When you realize that the bishop before you is the same man as the one in your vision, you understand that Saint Nicholas is the one who saved your life.

As a young adult and scholar, Nicholas chose early to forsake his family's wealth, focusing instead on his religious studies. Devoting his life to Christianity, he made many pilgrimages to the Holy Land, even though that meant crossing dangerous seas. Legends abound of his heroic rescues of ships and men, giving him the reputation of "Lord of the Seas."

In one such story, Nicholas prayed for deliverance when his ship encountered a violent storm. The terrified sailors were surprised and grateful when the seas calmed and the winds died down, but they were heartsick at the loss of one of their crew. In the worst of the gale, the man had slipped and fallen to his death while tightening ropes on the mast. After Nicholas prayed for him, he was miraculously restored to life with no injuries—two miracles in one day!

On another sea journey, the captain decided to make a detour to his own homeport. When a rogue storm threatened to capsize the whole ship, damaging the rudder beyond repair, Nicholas prayed. The ship righted itself, drifted directly to its original destination, and passengers and crew were safe. Even today, sailors may wish each other "safe passage" or "bon voyage," but just as often they say, "May Saint Nicholas have your tiller."

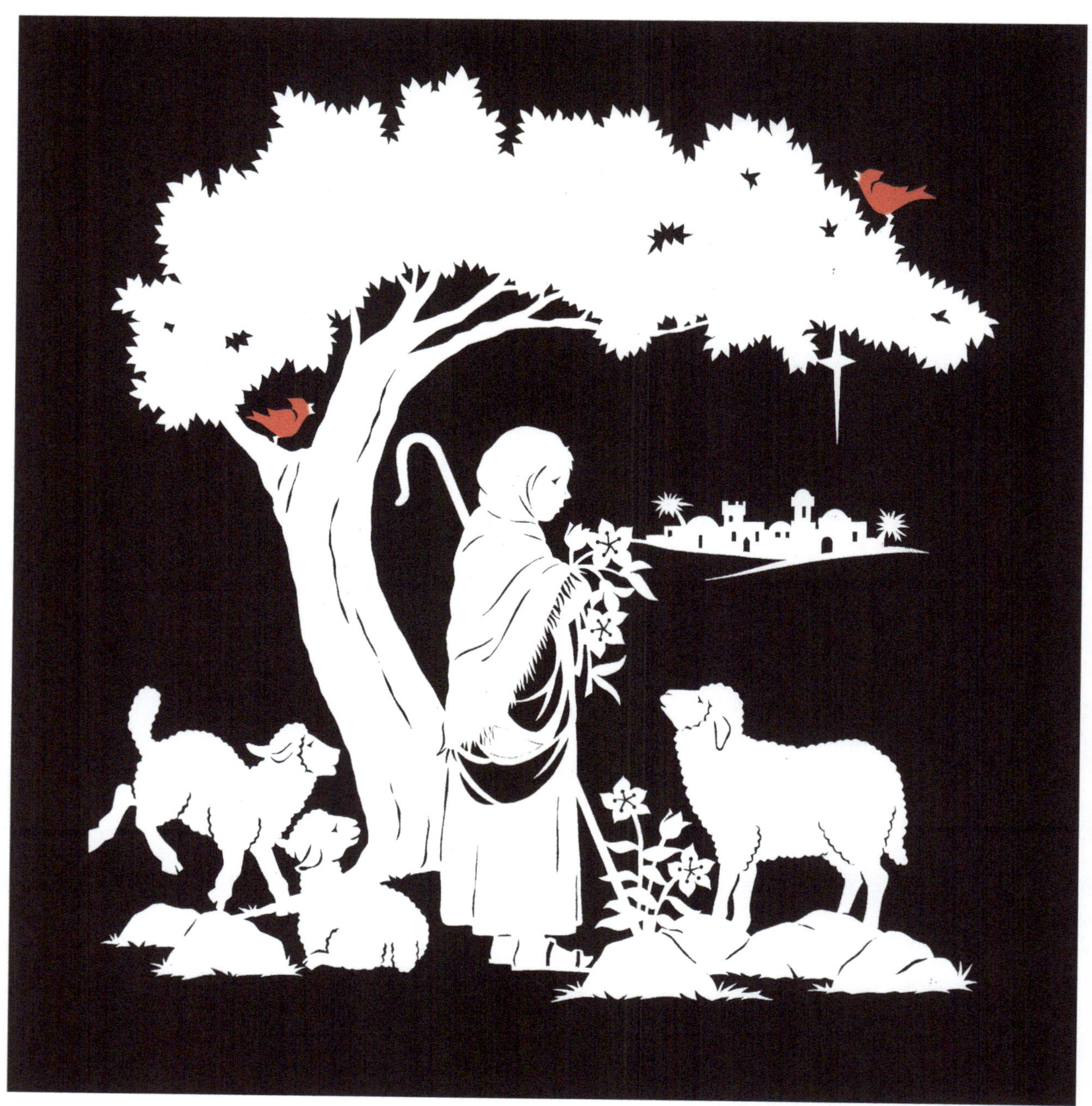

The Christmas Rose

The story of the Christmas rose, a winter flower that blooms in cold temperatures, combines real-life details with folklore and tells of the most meaningful gift of all, the one that comes from the heart.

The legend begins on dark lonely hills where shepherds, tending their sheep, are gathered around the night's fire to stay warm. It was a clear night, but cold. After the angel Gabriel appeared and told them of the birth of the Baby Jesus, sharing the message of peace and goodwill, the shepherds began their journey to Bethlehem. As they traveled down the hillside toward the city, following a brilliant star's rays of light, they were unaware of the young shepherdess, Madelon, following them silently in the shadows. She, too, wanted to bear witness to the new baby.

Traveling throughout the night, they eventually reached the stable where the newborn lay. The shepherds presented their humble gifts to Him—homemade barley bread, cheese, dried fruit, even a woolen blanket. The small shepherdess, hidden in the darkness outside, realized she had brought nothing to give.

She dropped to her knees in tears, heartbroken she had come so far with no gift. As the frozen ground thawed from her teardrops, and with the help of her guardian angel, silver-white roses grew up at her feet. It was a miracle! She now had the most perfect present, for these roses meant to her love and purity. She picked several stems of the blossoms, stepped out of the shadows, and offered her fresh bouquet to the most beautiful baby she had ever seen. Standing with her fellow shepherds in adoration, she felt profound peace, gratitude, and happiness.

When winter comes and the ground is frozen, remember to look for those pink-tipped, white blossoms, because gifts from the heart are as valuable as gold, frankincense or myrrh.

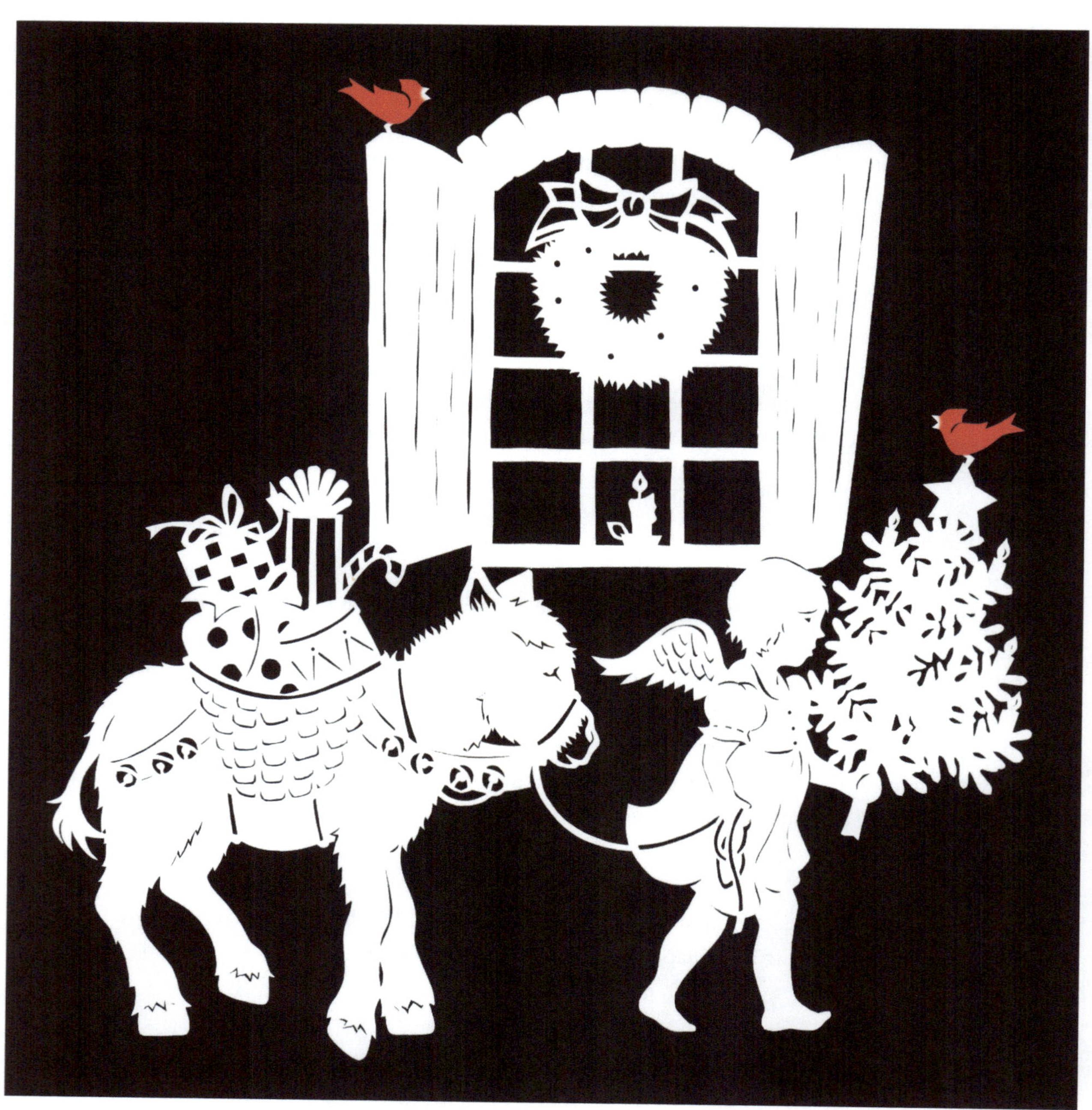

Bavaria's Christkindl

The legends of Saint Nicholas as the gift-giver were well established throughout Europe by the 16th century. Christian holiday celebrations at that time were a nice mix of ancient traditions and new religious devotions. St. Nicholas Day, when children received their much-anticipated presents, was celebrated on December 6, harkening back to the date of Saturnalia.

In the 1500s, though, church reformer Martin Luther disapproved of the Saint Nicholas celebrations. He was convinced that people were losing sight of the holiness of the time; he also did not want Protestants venerating saints. Still, Luther was clever enough to realize he could not just eliminate Saint Nicholas and all the established traditions that went along with him, so he began working on a replacement.

Eventually, the Protestant church introduced a new gift-giver—the Christkindl, or Christ Child—and changed the celebration to December 24 to coincide with the birth of Christ. The Bavarian people had trouble embracing the idea of the Baby Jesus giving the presents, so the Christkindl became more of an angel-like sprite, a heavenly child dressed in white; a clever twist to the myth of a child bringing gifts to Baby Jesus.

Today's legend tells of a golden-haired cherub arriving from heaven. A sweet-faced donkey carries gifts in baskets on its back for the cherub to deliver. Families are careful to keep candles lit in the windows to welcome the young angel into their homes and guide him or her safely. They leave one window open so that the angel can come in, quietly decorate the Christmas tree, and leave gilt-wrapped presents under it. Most families will have set up their carved heirloom manger scene near the tree that the angel is sure to admire. The angel rings a bell as he or she leaves so the family will know their celebrations can begin.

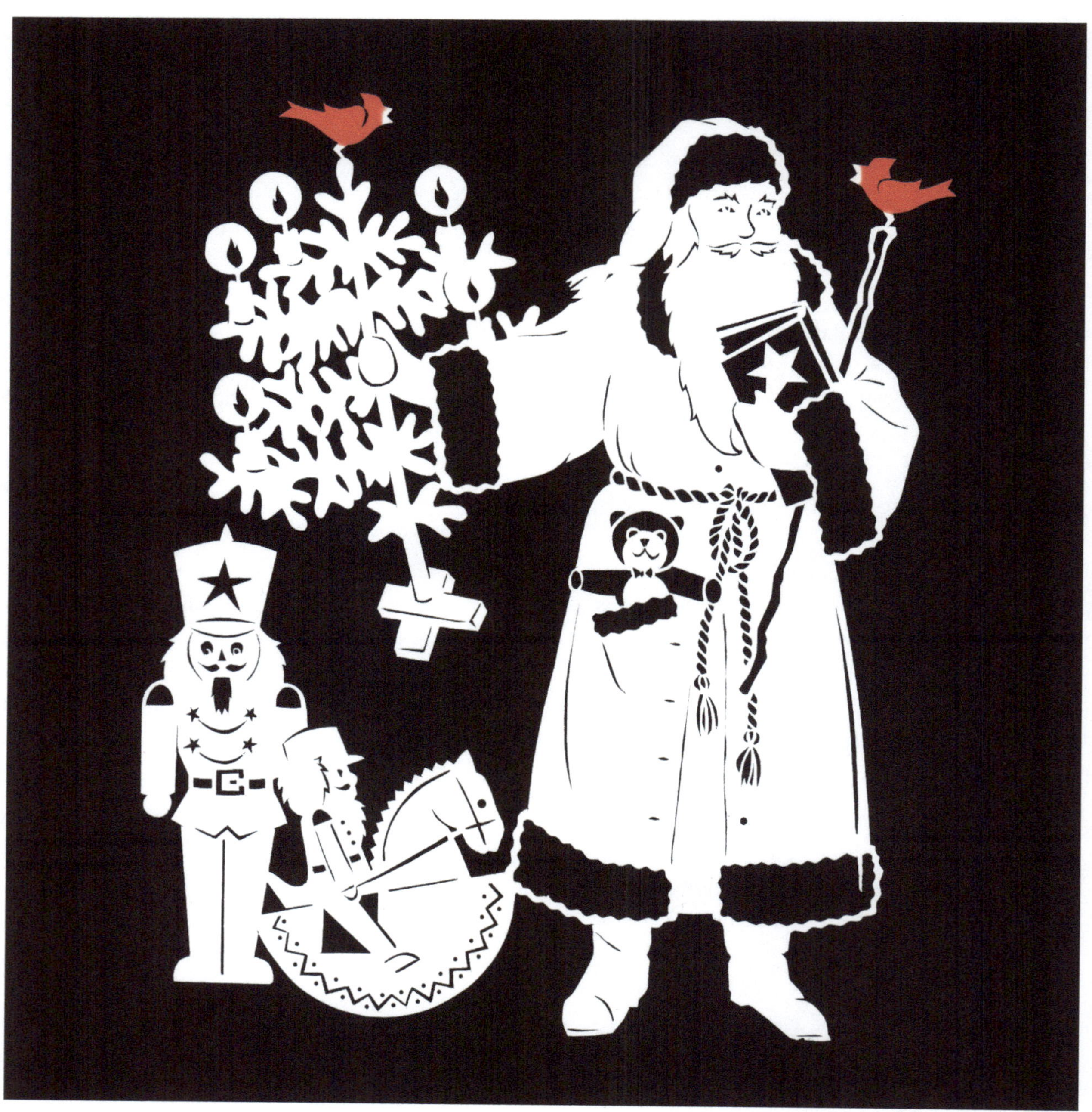

Germany's Weihnachtsmann

The magic of the winter holiday has been alive and well in Germany from pagan to Christian times and still today, with legends and lore, gift-givers galore.

One favorite legend says that in the dead of winter, the rivers of Germany turn to wine, the trees bear fruit, the mountains open up to reveal hidden gemstones, and church bells ring everywhere. BUT only the pure of heart can witness it all! Everything is richer and more bountiful at Christmastime.

Germany gift-givers include Sankt Nikolaus (Saint Nicholas), der Weihnachtsmann (Christmas Man), and Christkindl, all of whom pass out gifts to deserving children. On the other side of the coin are Krampus, Knecht Reprecht, and Pelzebock, who arrive with switches and coal to reprimand the children who weren't quite well-behaved.

December 6, the Day of Sankt Nikolaus (Saint Nicholas) begins the month of celebration. Children are careful to leave carrots on the windowsill or doorstep as a treat for the white horse bringing their first gift-giver. They put polished shoes or boots next to the plate of carrots to, hopefully, be filled with delicious nuts and fruits, candies and goodies. No one wants to find any coal, twigs, or potatoes!

Der Weihnachtsmann carries with him a giant book of names, which he consults before he disperses his gifts into the shoes. He also brings with him the evergreen tree that the parents will decorate later behind closed doors.

The rest of December includes the Advent wreath, with candles to light each Sunday, and the Advent calendar, with a window to open each day. German families put candles on the windowsills to "light the way" and of course cook, bake, and decorate in excited anticipation. On Christmas Eve, Christkindl arrives with more gifts and surprises. It is a month focused on family and community, joy and generosity.

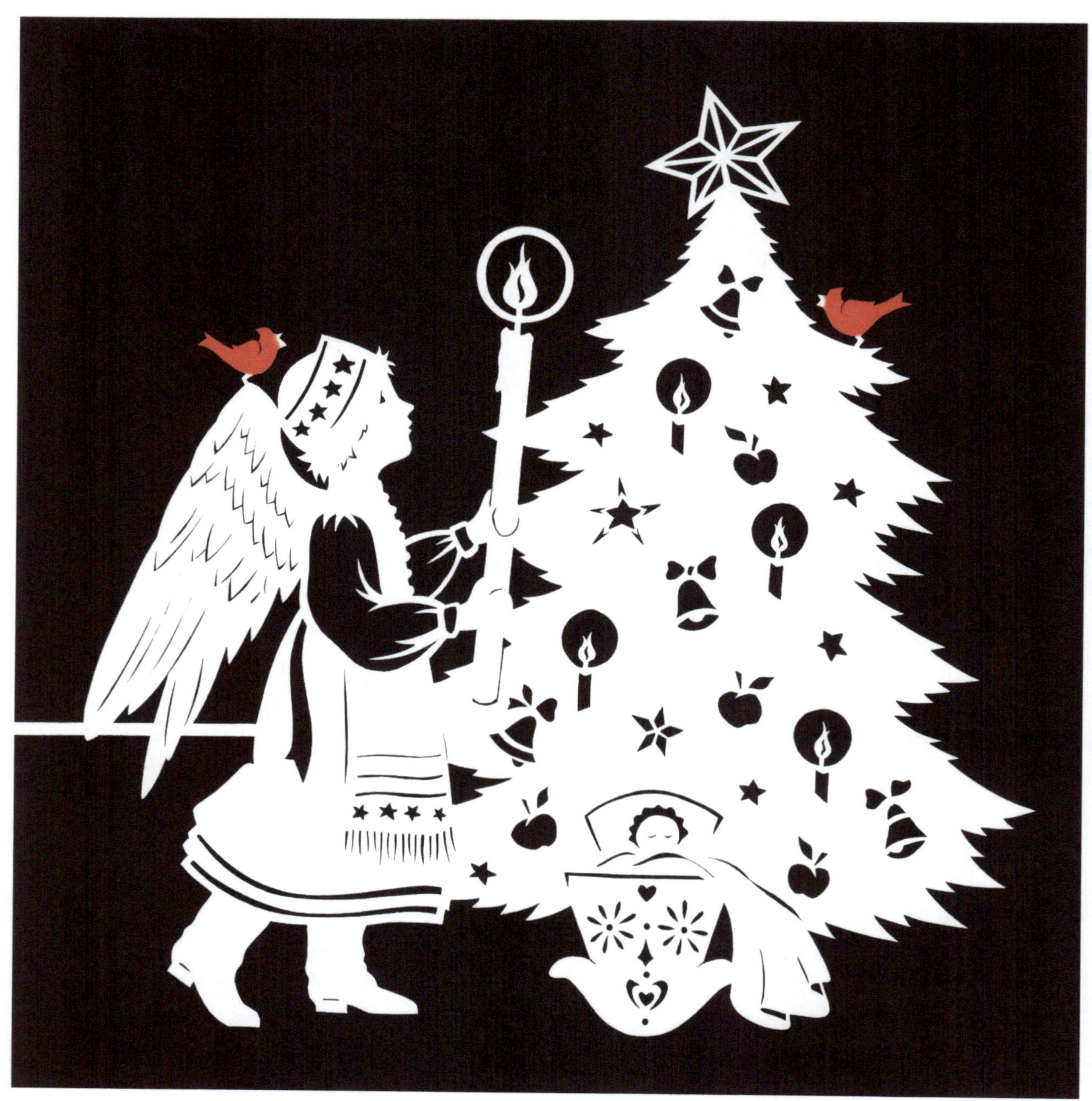

Hungary's Mikulas and Jezuska

The entire month of December is devoted to Christmas in Hungary. It begins with Advent, the time of expectant waiting, when people decorate candles and wreaths with red and gold ribbons to symbolize life and abundance.

On the eve of December 6th, children polish their boots, put them on the windowsill, and hope that during the night Mikulas, Saint Nicholas, will come. If they've been good, they'll get sweets, coins, small toys or books in their boots. If not so good, they might see onions, switches or coal. Often they will receive both, since no child can be ALL good or bad!

In mid-December the Bethlehem Plays, a mixture of Christmas pageant and caroling, boys and girls perform a short play recounting events of the Holy Night. Dressed as camel or Balthazar, lamb or shepherd, children bring their nativity from home to home, reminding everyone of the holiness of the Christmas legend.

On Christmas Eve, legend says that the Baby Jesus, Jezuska, and his angels come after dark and transform the family's living room into a wonderland. They bring in a Christmas tree and decorate it with embroidered felt and blown-glass ornaments, gingerbread cookies, and holiday candies called Szaalonchkor (chocolate and marzipan candy wrapped in gold and red foil). They tie real candles onto the fir tree branches. After putting presents around the tree, they light the candles before they leave. When morning comes, the room will smell like a pine forest and the lights will give the darkness a magical, ethereal glow.

In the morning, children have one last wait to endure. They may not go into the living room until they hear the bell that announces that the Baby Jesus and his angels have indeed come. Then they can rush in to enjoy the colors and light and fresh evergreen smells, not to mention all the wrapped packages!

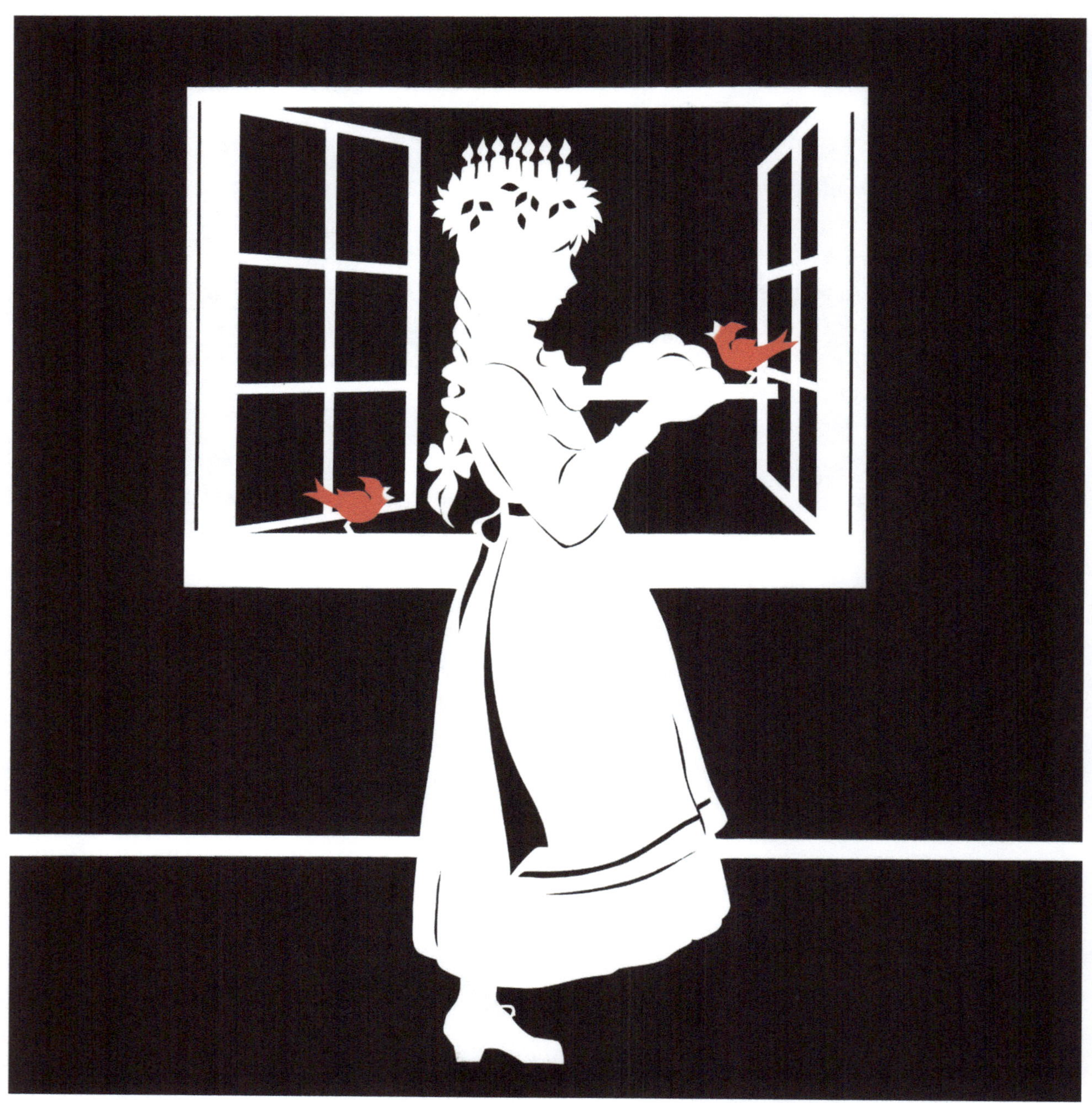

Sweden's Santa Lucia

The Swedish Yule begins before dawn on December 13 with the Festival of Santa Lucia, or the Festival of Lights. In the Julian calendar (before 1753), that date fell on the longest night of the year. This was once the night of ancient pagan, winter solstice rites, when people of northern Europe lit torches, bonfires, and oil lamps to light the darkness and express hope for their future.

Lucia was a young girl in Sicily around 300 AD, when Roman Emperor Diocletian was methodically persecuting all Christians. Lucia, dangerously, believed strongly in her faith. When her mother was cured of a dire illness at the sepulcher of St. Agatha, Lucia felt compelled to show her gratitude to her God. From that point on, she secretly traveled throughout the city at night, ministering to the needy. Her only source of light was a wreath of candles on her head showing her the way. Her legend was born.

Christianity did not come to faraway Sweden for about another 700 years, but tales of Lucia's generosity were by then well known in all of Europe. A favorite Swedish legend tells of a terrible famine at the height of winter. People near Lake Vannern were isolated and starving, with no hope of survival. A vision appeared, slowly moving across the frozen lake. A sailing ship with a beautiful young woman at the helm dressed all in white was gliding toward them. There was a radiant glow of light around her head. Miraculously, it was Saint Lucia with a ship full of food to save the village. The Swedes adopted Saint Lucia as their own symbol of hope.

Today in Sweden at Christmastime, it is customary for the eldest daughter of the house to wear a long white dress tied with a red sash to represent the saint. She also wears a crown made of lingonberry leaves with seven lit candles, echoing Lucia's nighttime rescue. She carries a tray of steaming hot coffee and gingerbread cookies or braided saffron buns (Lussekatt), and awakens the family to start their day of celebration.

Lucia's legend survived the Reformation, the change from the Julian to the Gregorian calendar, and years of cultural change in Sweden. A time of family joy and togetherness, the Festival of Lights symbolizes reverence for the past, appreciation for the present, and hope for the future.

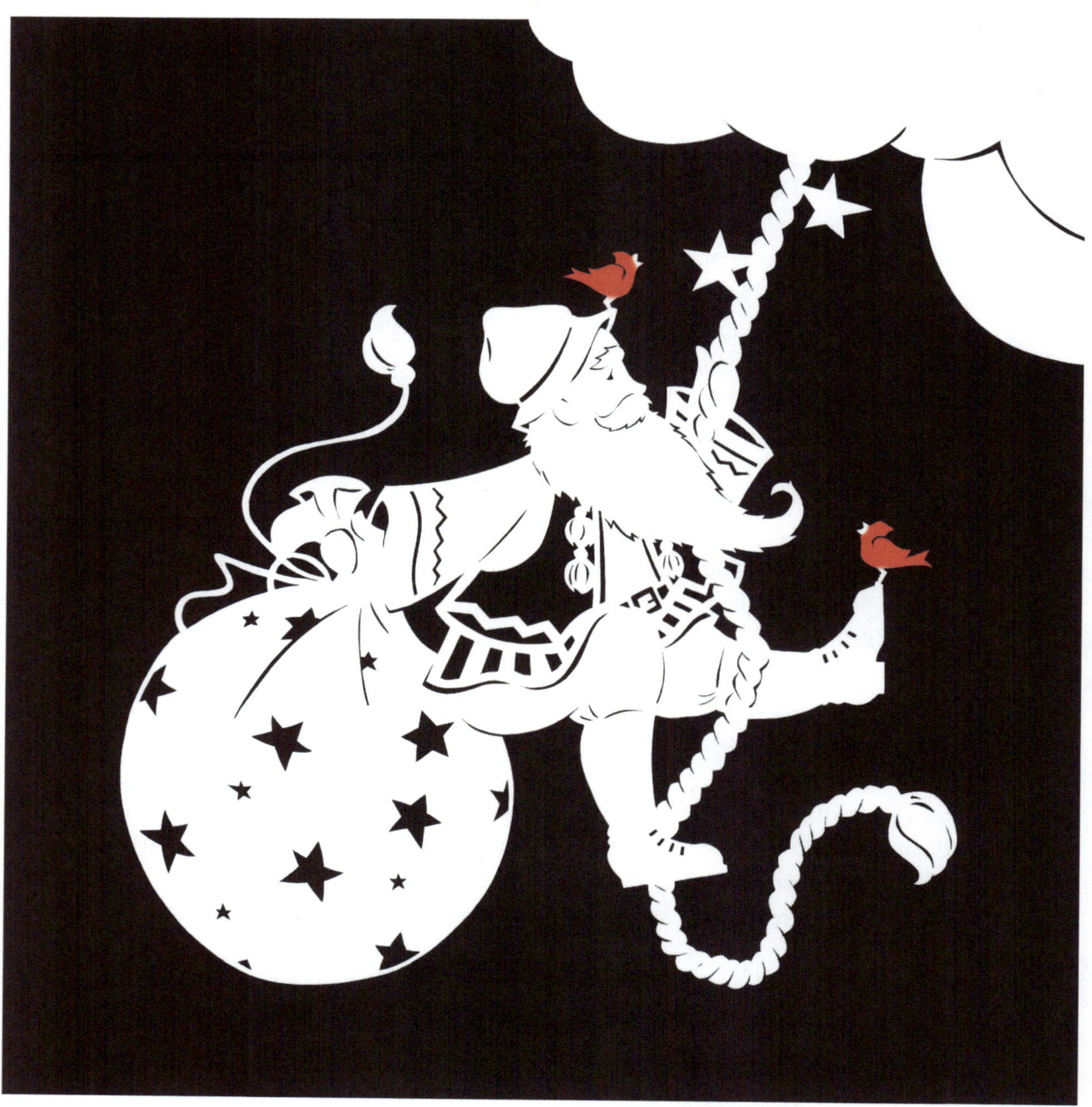

Czechoslovakia's Svaty Mikulas and Jezisek

Imagine Saint Nicholas, Svaty Mikulas in Czech, descending on a golden chord that stretches from heaven to earth! He has a basket strapped to his back overloaded with fruits, nuts, and presents. His two helpers follow him down—the angel and the devil (symbolizing the conflict of good and evil).

In Czechoslovakia, that is how the Christmas celebrations begin on December 5. You will see this threesome traveling to homes, town squares and holiday festivals, asking children how they behaved during the past year and if they deserve treats. Whether it is family or friends who dress up as these characters, it is a live play about good and evil and receiving rewards for positive choices.

Czech families also honor old superstitions that foretell one's life or love in the coming year. A favorite practice is to place a cut cherry branch in water in the beginning of December. If it blossoms by Christmas Eve, folklore says, the single girl of the family will probably be married by year's end, or the entire family will enjoy a year of good health and much fortune.

Weeks of celebrating culminate on Christmas Eve day, which is "Generous Day" in Czechoslovakia. Families decorate a fresh-cut tree with homemade and heirloom glass ornaments, prepare the elaborate evening feast, and anticipate the arrival of their gift-giver Jezisek.

The evening meal is traditionally a long one. It begins only after someone spots the first star in the darkening sky, in remembrance of the Holy Night. People include garlic in the meal (for protection), honey (to guard against evil), and mushrooms (for health and strength). It is a meal of togetherness and thanksgiving.

Anticipation rises all during dinner, because children know that when everyone is done, a bell will ring. The bell means that Jezisek has come! The story goes that he steals through an open window while the family is eating, silently leaving wrapped surprises under the tree for everyone.

Some legends say that Jezisek is part angel and part child, and lives in the mountains near Bozi Dar, not the North Pole. Whatever you believe, if you are a lucky Czech child, you have two gift-givers at Christmas.

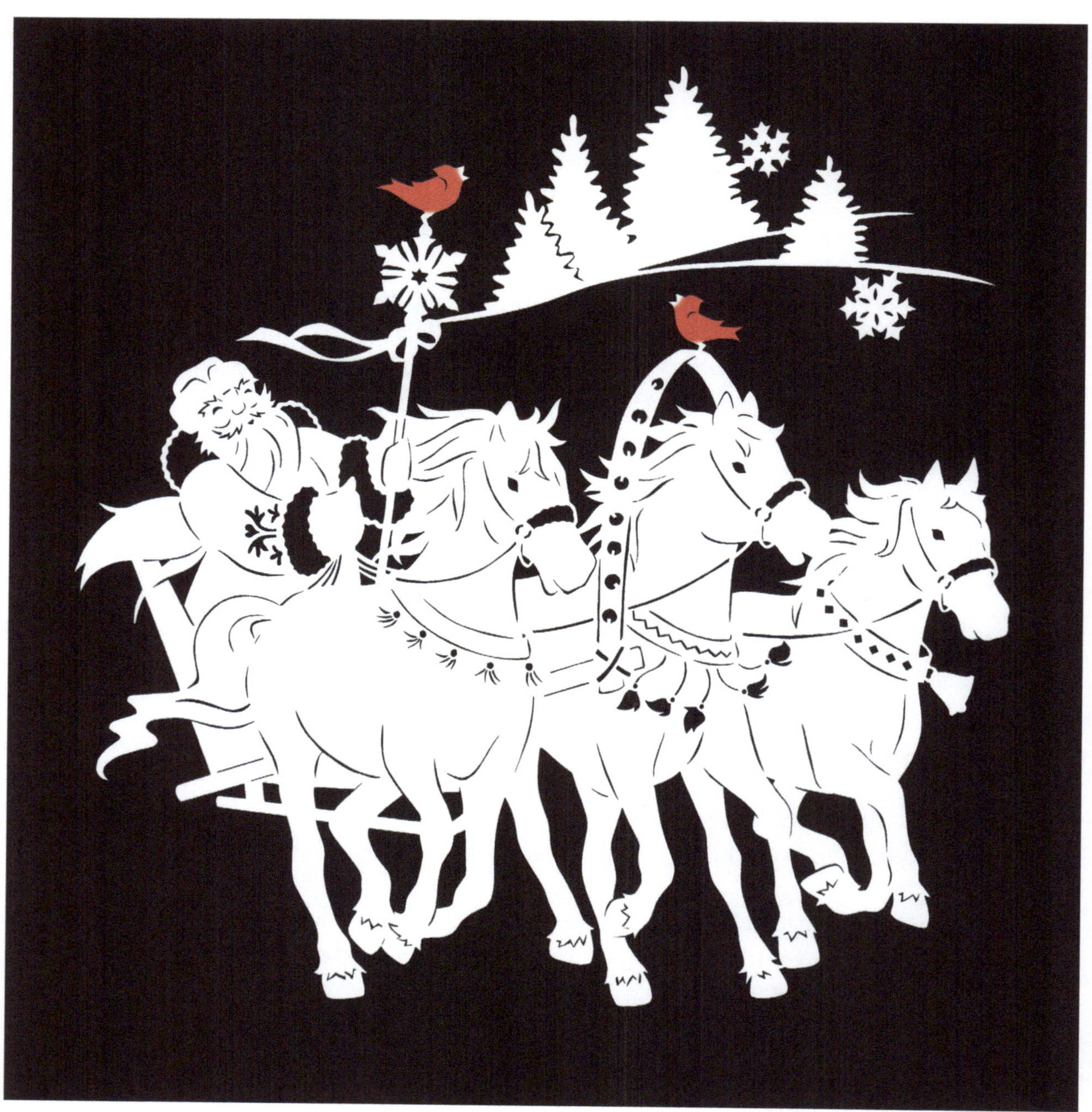

Russia's Ded Moroz

Russia's gift-giver has had many reincarnations. Before Christianity, Russians believed in many underworld spirits and gods and goddesses. Celebrations of the winter solstice included rituals and legends that explained the long cold season.

One god was Morozko, or Frost, and his myths vary. To some, he stole the warmth of the sun and ruined future crops with his frost, so people tried to charm him with gifts to get the sun back. Other people believed he was an evil sorcerer who froze children to ransom for gifts at the end of wintertime.

Amazingly, Morozko was also considered a kind and gentle hero who gave gifts to honest, hard-working people at the end of the year. These various legends spoke to the harshness of winter, the hope of the coming springtime, and the power of gift-giving. There was magic in Frost's stories.

Once Russia was Christianized and stories spread about the miracles of Saint Nicholas, he became Russia's patron saint and gift-giver. He was revered as the protector for the weak and downtrodden, the benefactor for the poor, and the one who would reward a virtuous life.

Frost reappeared as the gift-giver after the Reformation, when veneration of saints had been banned, and the Bolshevik Revolution, when religion in general was discouraged. The spirit of the holiday could not be dampened by politics, as people combined Frost and Saint Nicholas into Ded Moroz, or Grandfather Frost.

Ded Moroz arrives in a troika, or sled, pulled by three lively white horses. His hair and long beard are white to symbolize his age, the winter season, and happiness and wealth. He wears a long fur coat of blue (to separate him from the red-clad Santa Claus), and his fur hat is reminiscent of a Russian tsar's headgear. His magical staff, with its twisted handle and crystals, is always close by to ward away any evil spirits who may want to steal the presents he brings.

Ded Moroz and his granddaughter, Snegurochka, deliver their gifts in daylight and in person on New Year's Day, after their long journey from somewhere in the deep taiga forests of northern Russia.

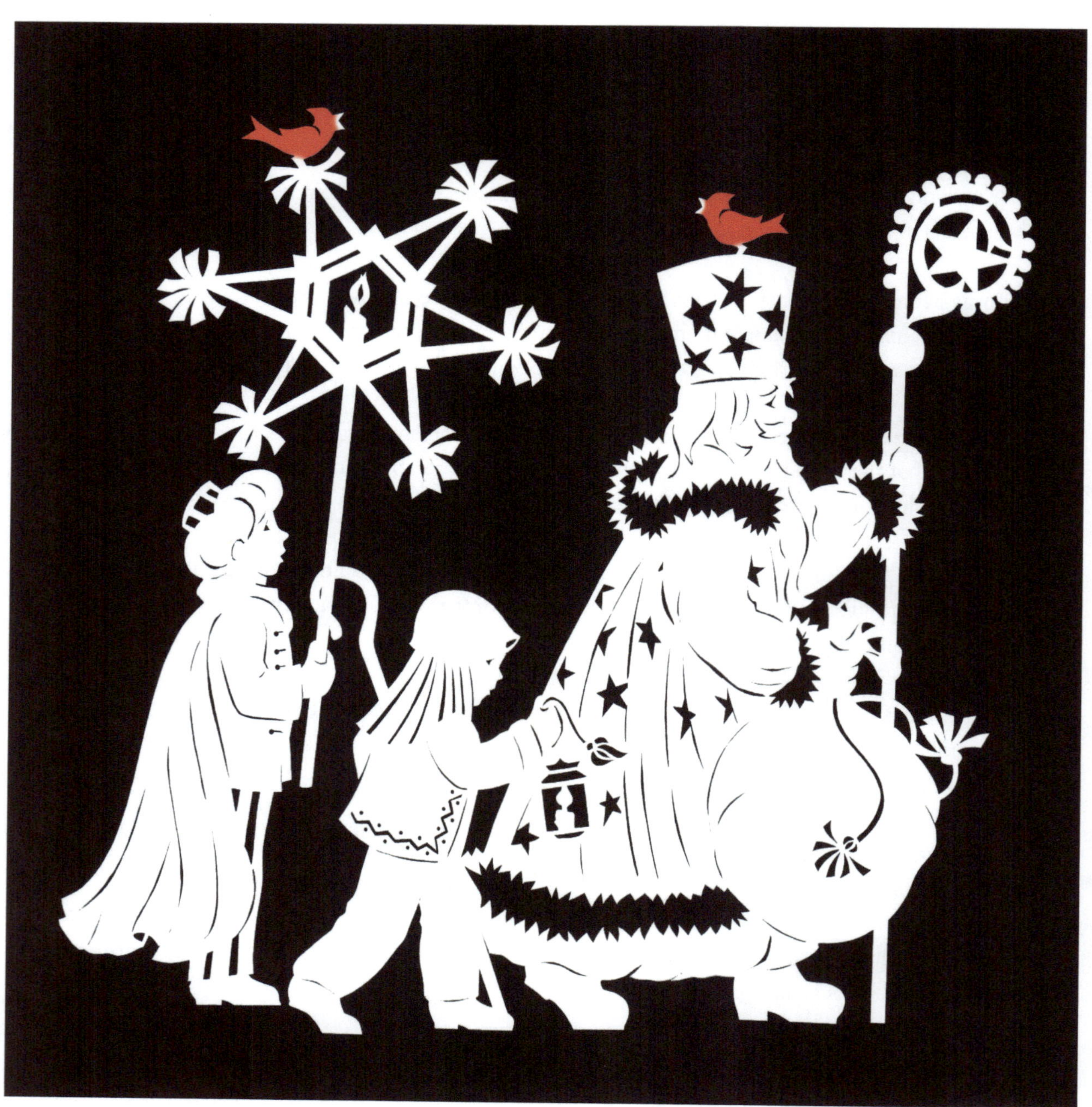

Poland's Swiety Mikolaj and Gwiazdor

Christmas in Poland is a month of celebrations, with two occasions for gift-giving: Saint Nicholas Day and Christmas Eve. Swiety Mikolaj, Saint Nicholas, is a saintly, dignified figure for the Polish. He is not a jolly, red-clad character, but dressed instead in a regal purple and gold bishop's robe, holding a pointed mitre and long crosier, or staff.

Saint Nicholas visits each home in early December, either on foot or astride his white horse. First he listens to each child review their catechism lessons for the past year. Once satisfied, he passes out surprises—holy cards, apples or oranges, and pierniki (honey and spice cookies with the saint's image impressed on them). It is both a serious and exciting night. The children's protector and patron saint has come to see them and congratulate them for being good.

The "real" Christmas starts with the sighting of the first star in the sky on Christmas Eve. ALL the month's preparations have led to this moment. Seeing the star, symbolizing the star of Bethlehem, means the end of the Advent fast, the start of holiday feasting, and the arrival of the Star Man (Gwiazdor). Legend holds that all gifts come from the stars!

Families set the dining table with great care, laying straw under the tablecloth as a remembrance of the manger and assembling an even number of chairs, including one for the Holy Child. They cook an odd number of foods, to assure a new year of good luck; superstition and tradition go hand in hand on this most special night of the year.

After dinner, a bell rings, announcing the arrival of Gwiazdor and his Star Boys!! It is a fantastic entourage, including the Star Man and boys dressed as various characters from the nativity scene. They sing Christmas carols as they parade into the house carrying a lighted candle or lantern. Gwiazdor the gift-giver shares treats with the children and visitors as everyone exchanges gifts.

The final celebration is the Mass of the Shepherds at midnight, where all give thanks for the blessings they have enjoyed.

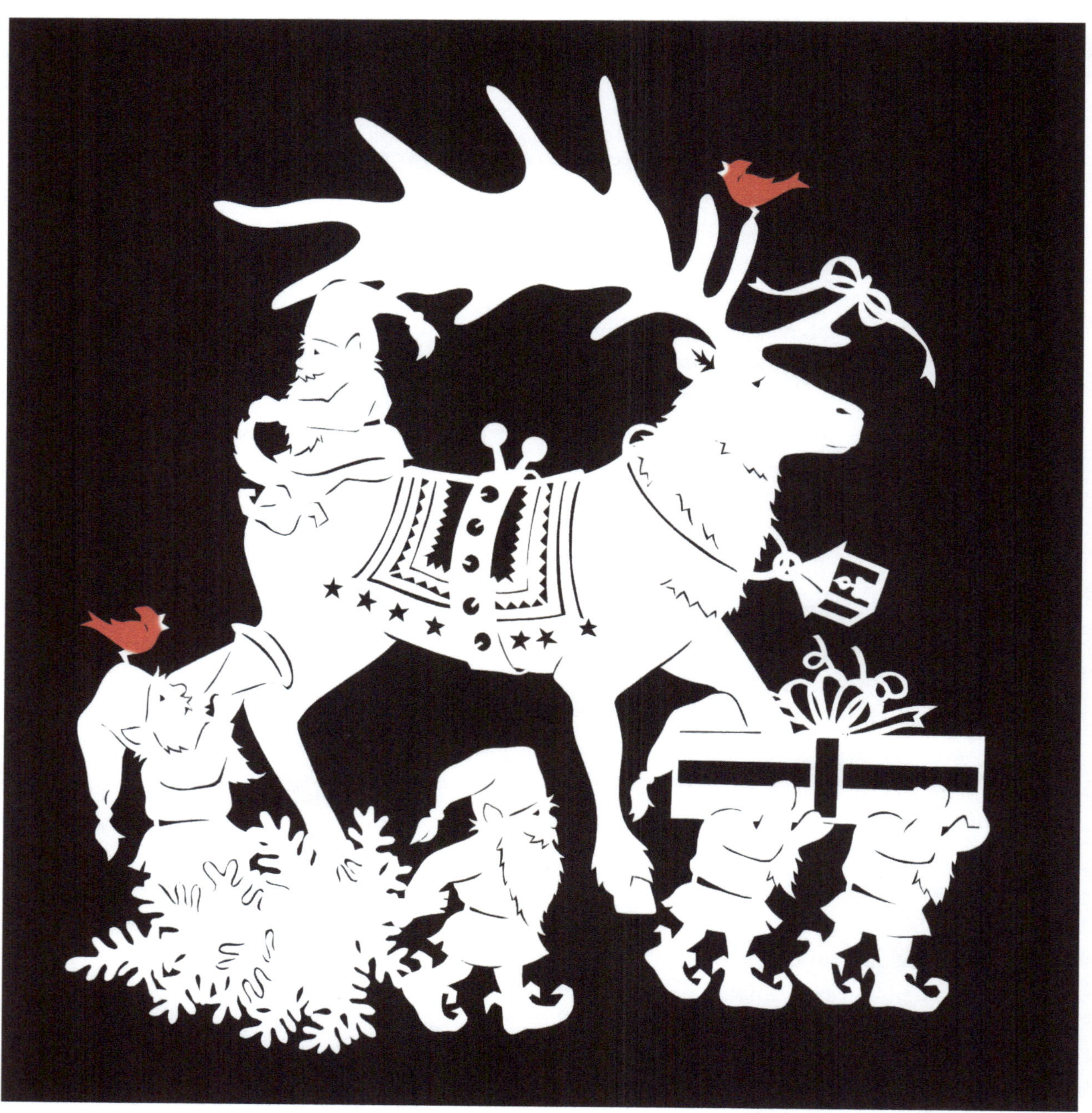

Ireland's Daidi na Hollag

Christmas in Ireland is a lovely blend of old and new. Ancient customs that date from pre-Christian days are still revered as important parts of the holiday. Whitewashing the outside of the house and cleaning everything inside until it shines was once how people tried to assist the gods in their battle against the powers of chaos. After Saint Patrick brought Christianity to Ireland in the 5th century, this custom evolved into purifying the home to honor the coming of the Christ Child.

Putting a candle on the windowsill perhaps echoes back to the winter solstice candle lighting to signify the return of the sun. Today, it is a symbolic way of welcoming the Holy Family on their route to Bethlehem.

Holly has been used as a symbol since the early Druids. The old Celts felt that it must be sacred, a favorite of the sun god, for it to stay green all year. The Romans gave sprigs of it for good luck and hung some on their doors to protect their home. Today, homes are decorated with holly, perhaps to provide a warm hiding place for leprechauns, and perhaps to honor the Holly King, who in pre-Christian days ruled from summer to winter solstice.

The legend of the Irish elk is still alive as well, even though the animal is extinct. The largest deer that ever lived, it stood seven feet tall at the shoulder, with 12-foot antlers from tip to tip, and weighed up to 1,300 pounds. Although it traveled across Eurasia, it has been dubbed the "Irish Elk" because so many of its remains have been preserved in their peat bogs. Is this elk the precursor for Santa's reindeer? Are the Irish leprechauns the models for Santa's helpers? Ask any Irish child!

Irish children, as everywhere, wish for their favorite things on Christmas morning, so they are careful to leave, perhaps, a pint of Guinness and a slice of mince pie to thank their nighttime guest San Nioclas (Saint Nicholas) or Daidi na Hollag (Father Christmas).

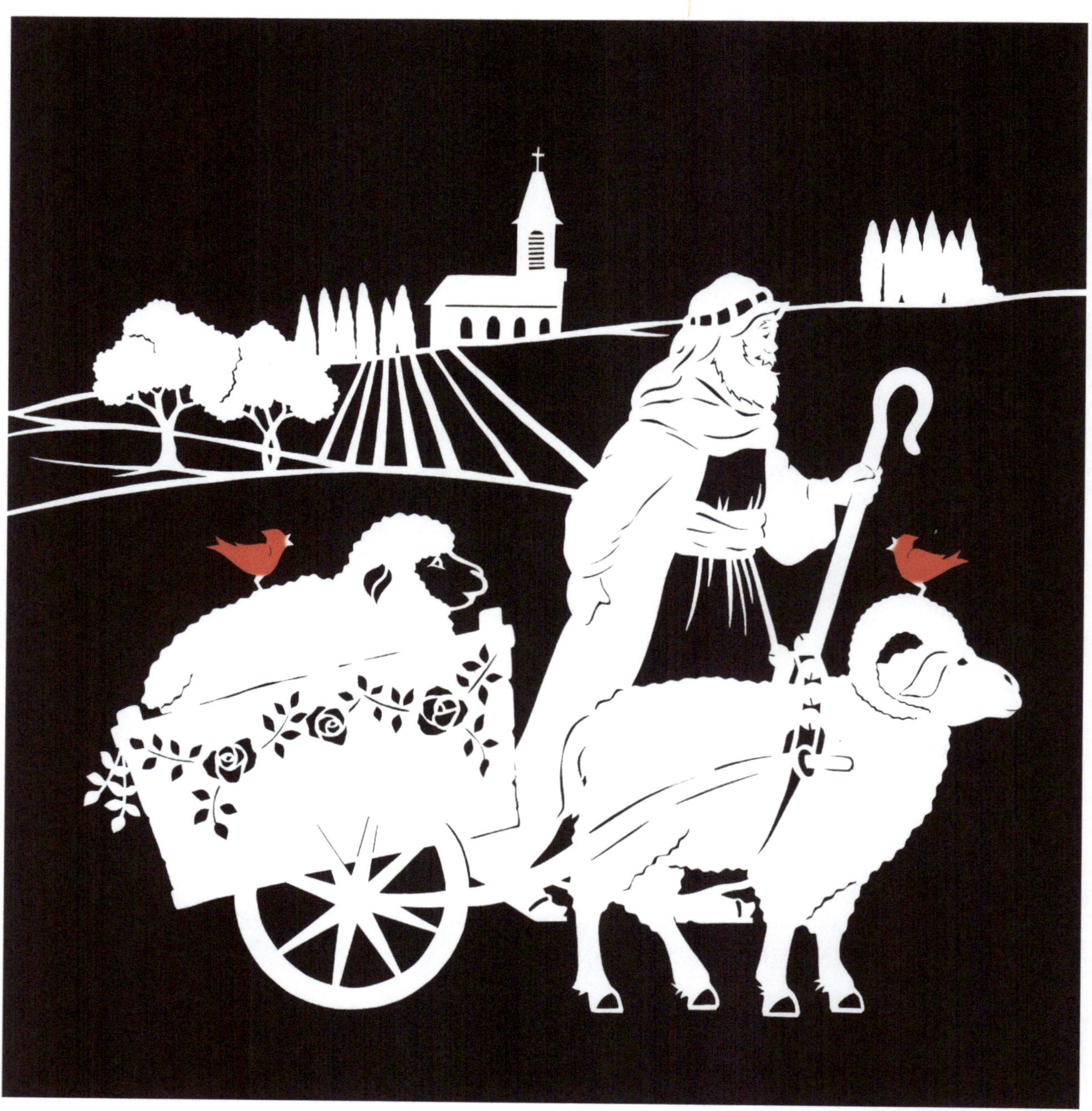

France's Pere Noel

In many regions of France, Christmas Eve celebrations include the Festival of the Shepherds, Fête des Bergers. A simple two-wheeled cart carrying a lamb and led by a ram is elaborately decorated with flowers and ribbons, candles and bells. Townspeople dressed as shepherds and shepherdesses lead a joyous procession, singing favorite carols accompanied by local musicians. The group circles the church so the congregation can join in. Mass begins only after the parade ends at the altar to offer the lamb to the priest in a symbolic gesture of their gift to the Christ Child, le Bebe.

Every family sets aside a special spot in their home for their heirloom nativity scene. In 1224, Saint Francis of Assisi first presented a re-creation of the Christmas story as a live play. What a wonderful way to "see" what happened on the Holy Night! The idea of a three-dimensional scene and characters captured the French imagination, and by the 1800s, nearly every family had wood or clay models of people and animals for their nativity. The figurines (santos or "little saints") are placed in and around a rough shed-like shelter, and adorned with fresh lichen, twigs and hay.

Today, historical accuracy sometimes takes a backseat to artistic license. You might see a figurine of the town's mayor standing between a camel and ox, the local baker beside the Magi, or a gardener and fisherman keeping company with the sheep and shepherds. As people assemble their own crèche scene in their home, they are expressing their strong emotional connection to the Christmas story.

In some parts of France, Father Christmas, or Pére Noel, arrives on the eve of Saint Nicholas Day (December sixth); elsewhere he comes on Christmas Eve. He wears a long red hooded robe trimmed in white fur and tied with a black belt. He carries his presents in a basket hanging on his shoulder. His companion is his trusted donkey Gui, and they deliver their surprises while the families are asleep. Children leave carrots for Gui and treats for Pére Noel, trusting that he will reward all their good behavior with gifts from his basket.

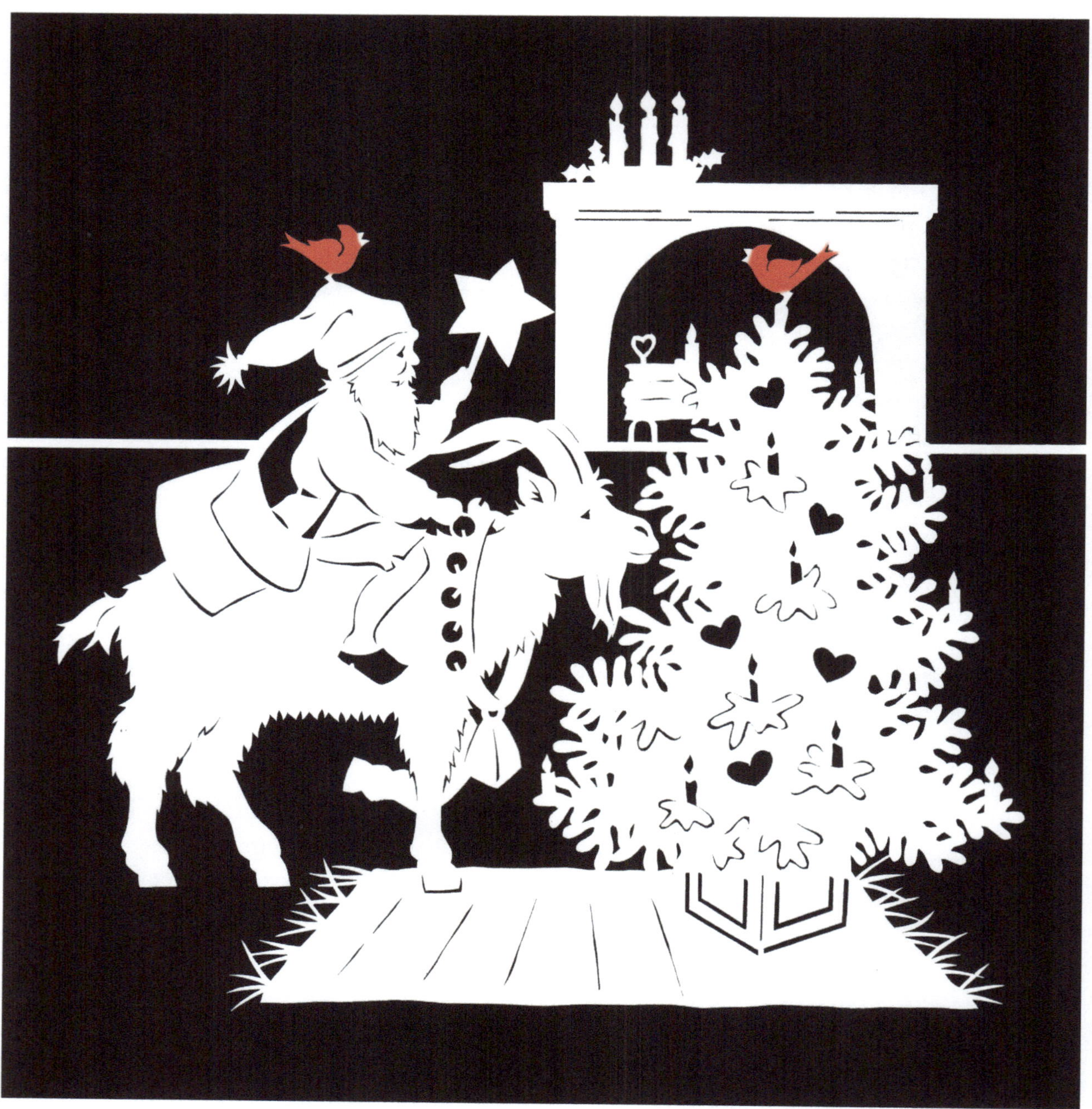

Denmark's Nisse

Despite long nights and frigid weather, Christmas is a jubilant time of year in Denmark. Its stories and traditions are a unique interweaving of Nordic myths and Christian teachings and beliefs, with special emphasis on family and community.

When the idea of a decorated evergreen tree became widespread in Europe, Danes wholeheartedly embraced it. Handmade ornaments became a home industry. Similarly, the giving and lighting of Christmas candles symbolized hope in Denmark's long, dark winter. They were also given to the poor as charity, to show the way for travelers, and to count the days until December 25th.

But everyone's favorite Christmas tradition is probably Nisse. In the earliest stories, this character was a little, old gnomish man who lived in the dark spaces of one's home or barn (in lofts or attics, under stairways). Nisse, or Tomte in Sweden, was the family caretaker who watched over children, adults, and animals. An impish personality, he was prone to trickery if he got bored or felt unappreciated. Just for fun, he just might hide things, tie the cows' tails together, or turn things upside down! The nighttime was his daytime and any morning surprises were always Nisse's doing.

Over time, Nisse came to be closely associated with Christmas, and so he became a gift-giver. He is held in great esteem in spite of, or because of, his tricks. He still lives in dark spaces and is still very close to the family cat (the only one able to see him). He wears gray homespun clothing, a red long-tailed knit cap, red stockings, and white clogs. Late on Christmas Eve, he arrives either on a present-laden sled pulled by a goat (a reference to the god, Thor, whose chariot was pulled by two goats) or on foot, dragging his bag of presents behind him in the snow.

Nisse comes through the front door and leaves all the presents under the Christmas tree, unless he wants to have some fun and hides some in strange places. Then he happily enjoys some cinnamon-sprinkled rice pudding, left by the family to appease his impish side, to thank him, and to fortify him for his night's work.

This cheerful elf is the personification of Christmas spirit—the season of love, joy, generosity and humor.

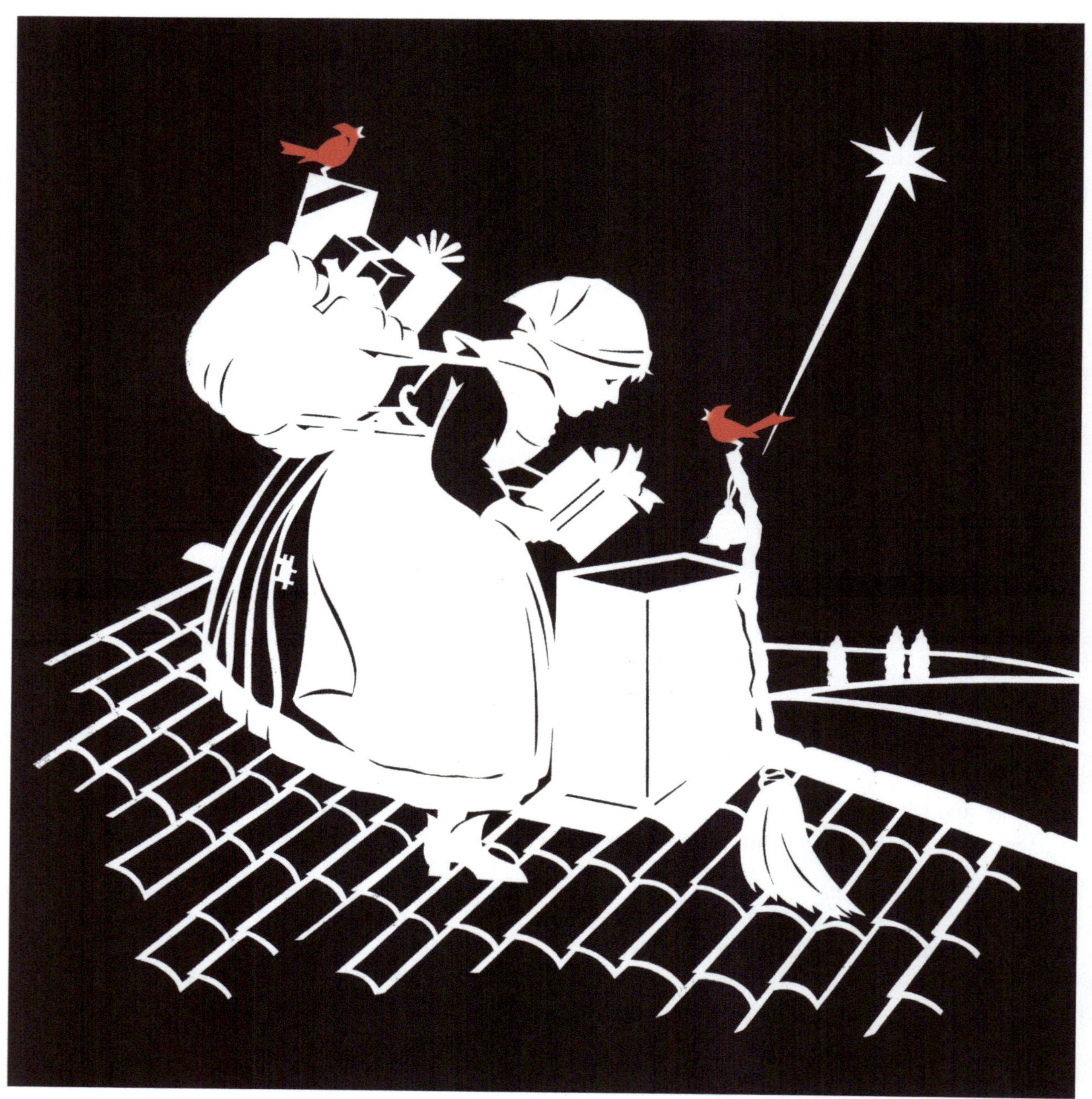

Italy's Lady Befana

The legend of Italy's gift-giver, Lady Befana, has its roots in pagan legends about the hearth goddess, but she has been Christianized enough so that her magical presence coincides with the stories of today's Christmastime. Tied to the solstice celebrations that honored the end of the current year and beginning of the next, the journey of Lady Befana (derived from the Italian name for Epiphany, epifania) is celebrated on the eve of January 6th, Three Kings Day.

The story tells of a lonely old woman who had spent the day cleaning her modest cottage. She was still sweeping the rough wooden floor toward evening. She was tired and hungry, and her dinner of beans and bread was ready.

Then there was a knock at the door. In no mood for company, the old woman opened the door to see three very foreign-looking men in splendid robes. They said they had traveled a great distance, following the brightest star in the sky, looking for the newborn king in Bethlehem. The star, unfortunately, had dimmed and they had lost their way. They were hoping she could help them.

She hadn't finished her housework, she didn't know anything about a new baby, and she didn't know these men. She shut the door and watched them leave, peeking from behind the window's heavy curtains.

All night she thought of nothing but her exotic visitors, and finally had a change of heart. Grabbing some humble gifts she left her cottage, still in her apron and carrying her broom. Unfortunately, as hard as she looked and as far as she went she could not find them…or the baby they had spoken of.

Today, it is said that Lady Befana still travels from home to home on her broom, looking for the Baby Jesus so that she can finally deliver her gifts. If a home has a child or children, she sends the gifts down the chimney and leaves the small ones in the stockings hanging from the hearth or bedsteads. Her visits are rewarded with a small glass of wine and a plate of regional goodies—a nice change from bread and beans!

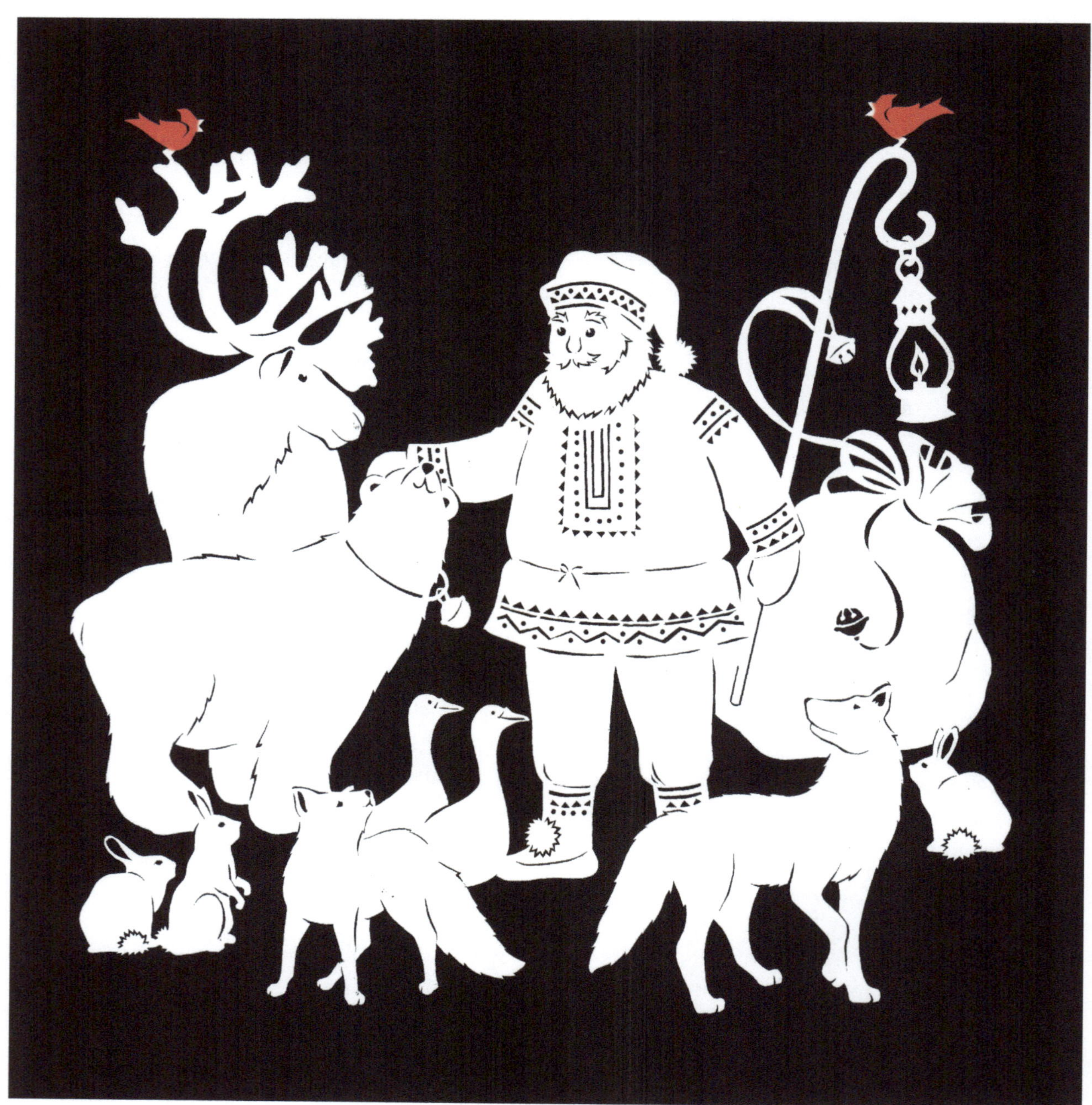

Finland's Joulupukki

In 1885 the American political journalist, Thomas Nast, first wrote that Santa Claus lived at the North Pole. (He actually meant the magnetic north pole located somewhere in Canada, not the geographic North Pole). With the current events of his day and the new explorations of the Arctic, the Land of Perpetual Snow was the perfect spot to locate the beloved gift-giver's imaginary base.

Or so it seemed. In the 1930s, the believers in Finland had a problem with this location.

The Finnish gift-giver is Joulupukki, meaning "Yule Goat." The original pagan lore told of a character, wearing Viking-like headgear with horns, whose job it was to protect the families of the area from evil spirits. At Christmastime, rather than giving out presents, he demanded offerings from everyone under his protection. He was the gift-receiver rather than the gift-giver who wanted to be rewarded for his year's hard work. A rather abrasive sort, he was appreciated, but feared.

Joulupukki eventually assumed a kinder persona, taken from the legend of the European Saint Nicholas. This new and more generous character rewarded "good" children with gifts on Christmas Eve. Interestingly, Joulupukki came through the front door rather than down through the chimney.

Markus Rautio of the radio show "Children's Hour with Uncle Markus" added his own twist the way Thomas Nast did. He announced that Joulupukki actually lived on Lapland's Korvatunturi Mountain, not at the North Pole. He felt it was the perfect spot. It was above the Arctic Circle, in a country where reindeer roamed freely. The snow-covered mountain was above the tree line and shaped like two giant rabbit ears pointing into the sky, so that Joulupukki could easily hear all the wishes of the good boys and girls around the world.

In modern Western folklore, it is generally universal that the gift-giver lives in a land of snowy whiteness where many animals are white, too. Whether it is the land of reindeer, caribou, or Finnish deer, we can all imagine busy elves or gnomes building toys and making lists somewhere in the cold, icy north.

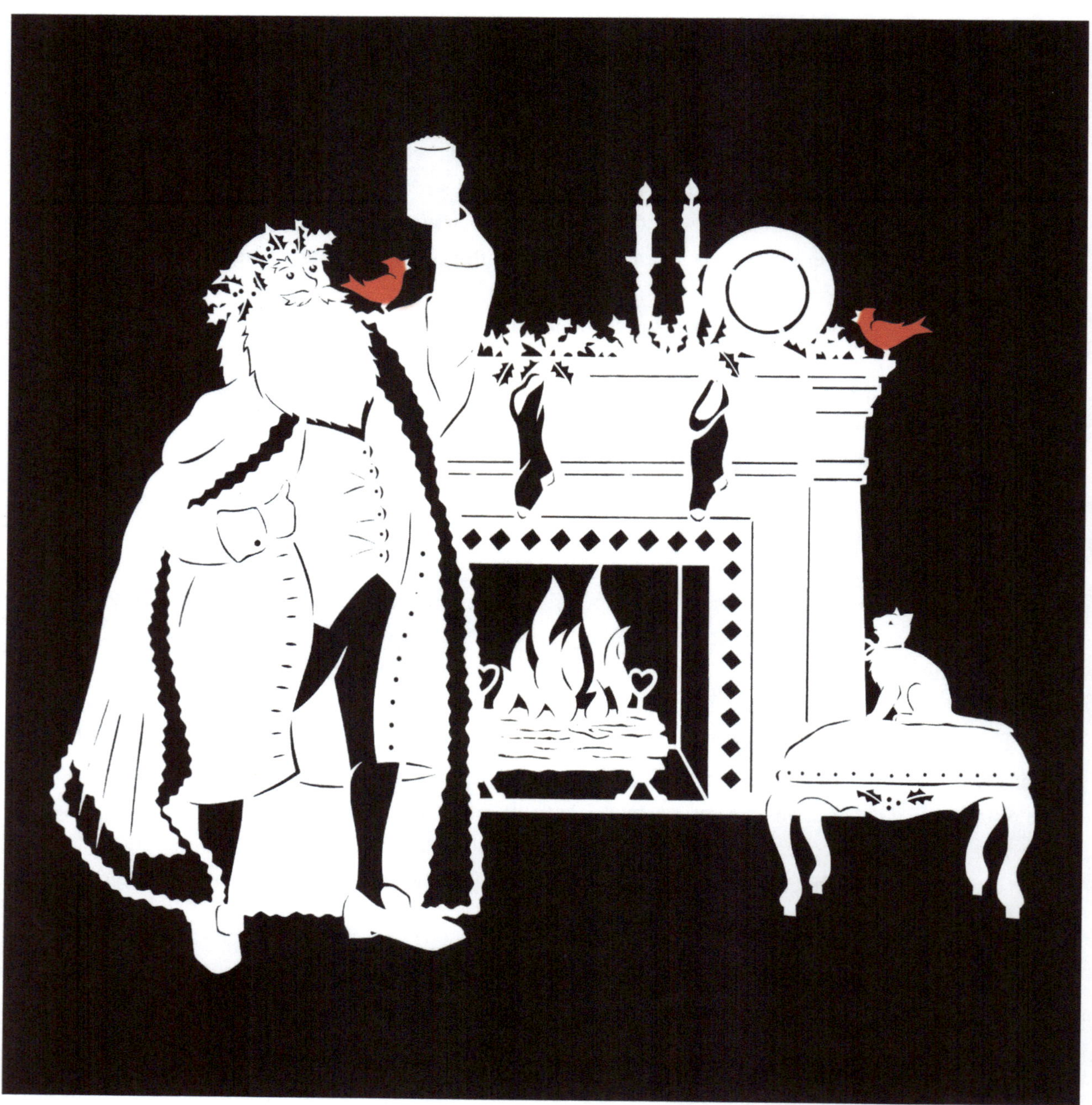

England's Father Christmas

Winter legends in England began as ways to cope with and explain the hardships and extremes of that season. Then, as Christianity spread through Europe, belief in the protective gods of the early Saxon and Viking tribes gradually gave way to Christian beliefs and gift-givers.

For 5th and 6th century Saxons, the most important gift would have been the end of winter. To help ensure that, they began a play acting tradition in which a neighbor would be invited to one's home to act the part of Winter. Wearing a hat or crown to be in character, he was generously fed and entertained. People believed that if Winter was treated well, surely he would provide them with warm weather and a sense of renewal.

A few centuries later, the Vikings in England believed in Odin, the father of all gods. In winter, families and friends gathered around the hearth to talk about their lives. They believed Odin came down from the heavens to join these discussions, so they showed generosity to any stranger in hopes that he was Odin in disguise. If he were treated well, perhaps he would return the favor by bestowing happiness and abundance upon them. The Norman invasion of England in 1066 brought stories of a new gift-giver, Saint Nicholas, a real person who answered prayers and brought surprise gifts.

During the 18th century, local theater productions portrayed a bearded man, dressed in a long green fur-lined robe to celebrate the season. The personification of peace and good will, he was named Father Christmas.

We all know how effectively Charles Dickens portrayed Father Christmas, especially in his classic *A Christmas Carol*. The Ghost of Christmas Present, in particular, is the essence of good cheer. His appearance was now closer to a very jovial Holly King with red hair, long green robe, and holly crown but he was still given the role of guest to be entertained and catered to.

The changes made to the Christmas traditions during the Victorian Era remain today. The emphasis was shifting more and more toward nurturing children's positive perceptions and experiences of Christmas. Father Christmas evolved from a visitor who came to listen and be entertained to one who brought presents. He is not Saint Nicholas, but more of a secular holiday gift-giver.

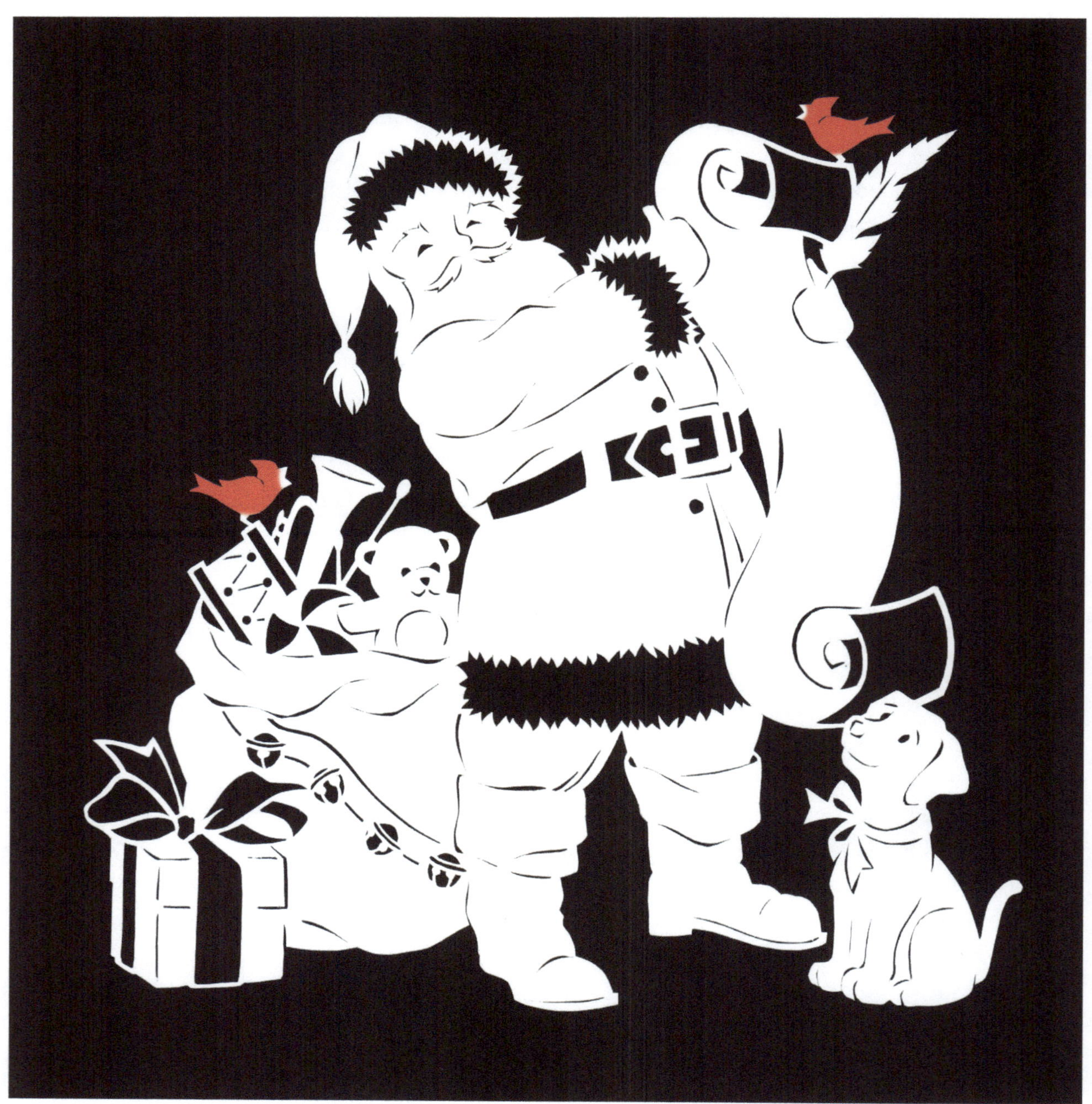

America's Santa Claus

The American author Washington Irving began the Santa Claus incarnation in the early 1800s. The name was a natural phonetic change from the German Sankt Niklaus and the Dutch SinterKlaas. Irving's gift-giver was an elfish Dutchman with a broad-brimmed hat, huge breeches, and a clay pipe. He rode over the treetops and rooftops in a wagon pulled by one reindeer, and dropped gifts down the chimneys as he flew over. He was a natural result of America's tremendous energy, pride, and creativity.

By 1844, book publishing and magazine printing, advertising, and marketing were well established. *The Children's Friend* printed Christmas stories and showed a "Santeclaus" similar to Mr. Irving's. The jolly old elf made famous in "The Night Before Christmas" was also widely popular. *Harper's Weekly* showed Thomas Nast's own illustration and story of a rotund Santa with a flowing beard, fur-trimmed garments, and a clay pipe. This gift-giver lived at the North Pole until Christmas Eve night, when his eight reindeer pulled a sleigh across the sky, delivering Santa and his sack of presents from rooftop to rooftop.

When President Grant signed into law a bill making Christmas a civil holiday in 1870, he paved the way for Santa Claus. Both the holiday and the gift-giver were now being promoted through children's storybooks and women's homemaking magazines. Santa Claus was a perfect marketing and merchandising tool, with authors and illustrators of every stripe getting on the bandwagon. In the 1920s, N.C. Wyeth's and Norman Rockwell's memorable images set the stage for Haddon Sundblom's Coca-Cola advertising icon of the 1930s, the Santa we still see most often today.

As modern as he may be, even our Santa retains a hint of very old legends and myths. Take his near-impossible route down the chimney, for example. Primitive beliefs hold that the chimney and hearth were where elves and fairies brought gifts to the home. Similarly, the pre-Christian Norse Odin entered the houses on the solstice through the chimneys. The Italian Lady Befana is always shown as soot-covered from her travels down the chimneys. So, however improbable, our American Santa Claus and his huge sack come inside the same way!

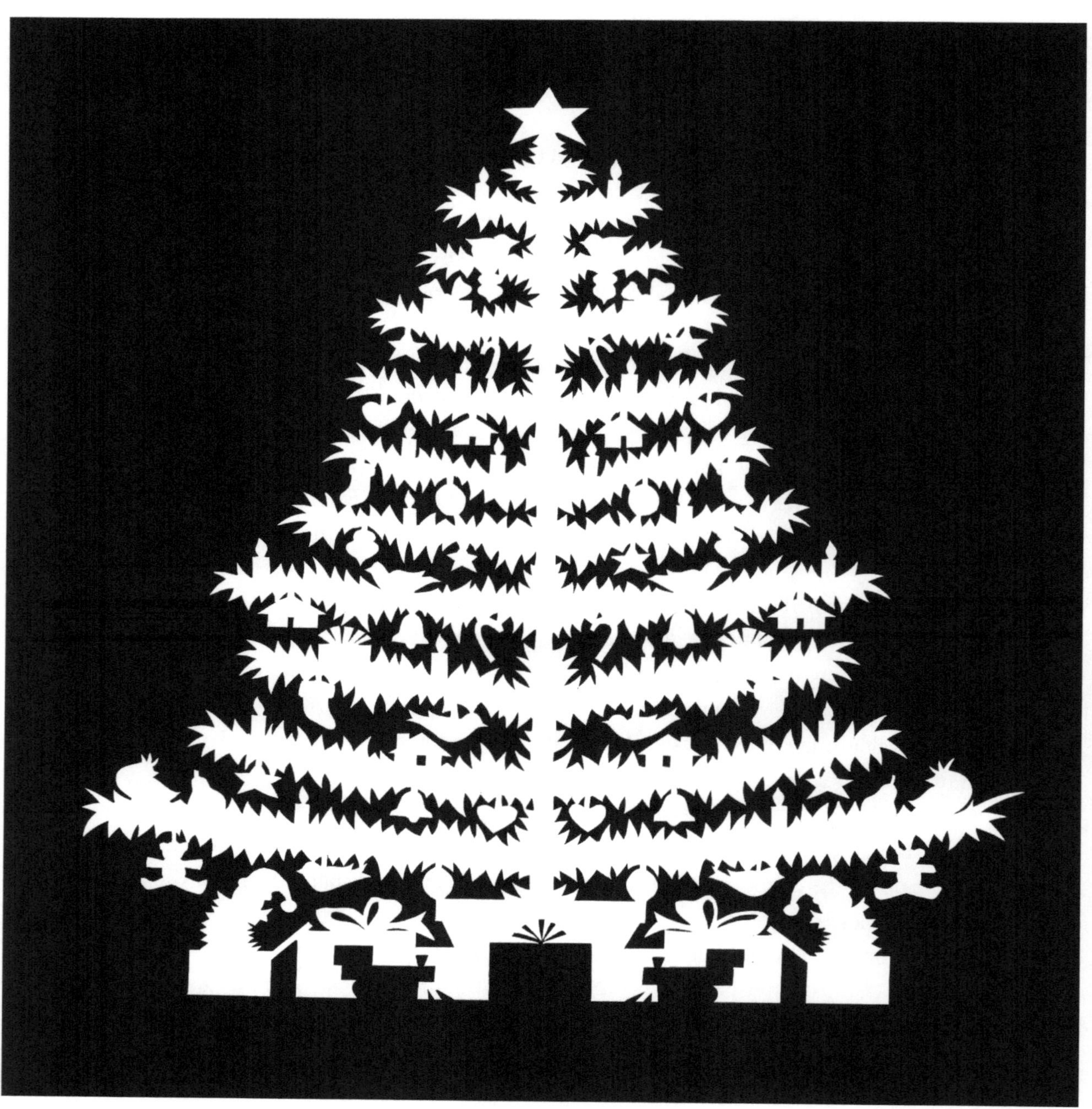

The Christmas Tree

The evergreen tree has been central to winter holiday celebrating and gift-giving since ancient peoples believed that a tree-spirit of everlasting life lived inside. People brought fir boughs into their home to protect their family from evil spirits and illness and to freshen the air.

In early Rome, the Saturnalia festivals of the solstice were a time of revelry, visiting friends, and giving gifts. People shared coins for prosperity, pastries for happiness, and lamps or candles to light one's journey through life. They also decorated their lintels and temples with live fir branches, to remind them of all the green plants that would grow again when the sun god regained his health in spring.

Christianity brought new mythologies, including references to the Tree of Life and the Garden of Eden. Legend says that Martin Luther created the first illuminated Christmas tree in 1500. Walking home late on Christmas Eve, he was entranced by the brilliance of the stars he could see twinkling amidst the evergreens in the dark winter sky. To share that sense of awe and reverence for God's gifts, Luther erected a tree in the family living room and wired real candles on all the branches.

In 1846, *Illustrated London News* featured Queen Victoria and Prince Albert with their children around a decorated tree in Windsor Castle, gifts galore underneath the branches. Families in the High Victorian Era quickly took to the idea, and soon a decorated fir tree was the centerpiece in many homes at Christmas.

Christmas tree traditions came to America with the Hessian soldiers and thousands of German immigrants. The early settlers made all their tree decorations—quilled snowflakes, folded-paper stars, sewn pouches for secret gifts, beaded ornaments, small paper baskets filled with sugared almonds and, of course, the beautiful cornhusk angel for the treetop. Later, glass ornaments were imported from Germany to add even more sparkle and magic.

However it is decorated, the Christmas tree has been a treasured part of our celebrations for hundreds of years, a symbol of joy, gratitude, and love. It is, after all, the place where so many gift-givers leave their surprises.

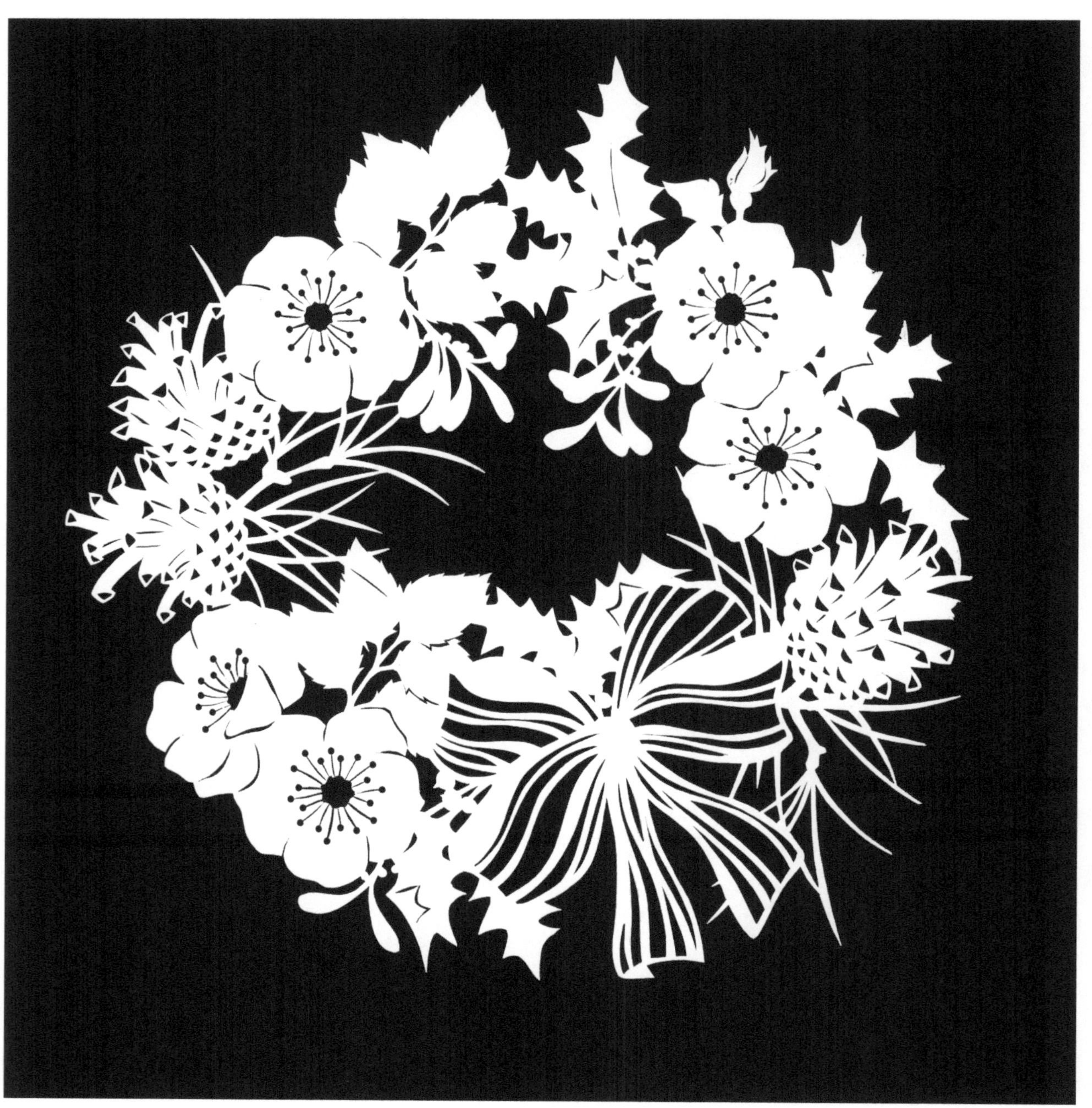

The Christmas Wreath

Today, holiday wreaths are a joyful sign, welcoming the gift-giver's generosity and love at Christmastime. But these festive decorations that adorn our doors and mantels are heir to centuries of myths and traditions. Its circular shape, having no beginning and no end, is a symbol of infinity or eternity, and also represents the cycles of life, nature, and the seasons.

Greeks and Romans awarded an olive wreath to the victors of all competitions. Druids used a wreath of evergreens to symbolize nature's strength against the ravages of winter. Scandinavians put candles on their wreaths to encourage the sun god to reappear once again in spring. To Christians, the wreath symbolized the crown of thorns worn by Jesus, as well as the resurrection and eternal life.

Evergreens were sacred in many early cultures, representing victory over difficulties, strength in adversity, and endurance and resilience. Holly was thought to house good spirits who kept the evil ones away. Early Romans believed holly, given as gifts at Saturnalia, protected one's home. The Celts thought that holly represented life and rebirth, a symbol of their Holly King who had saved an entire population. One Christian legend says that holly grew leaves out of season to hide the Holy Family from Herod's soldiers. To show His appreciation, the plant has stayed forever green.

Mistletoe has mystical appeal, too, believed to provide protection and ensure prosperity. Considered a plant of peace by the Druids, it also served as a sign of truce between antagonists. People in the Middle Ages believed it could protect the home, family, and even barns and animals. The Victorian tradition of kissing under a ball of mistletoe as a sign of friendship and goodwill soon changed to a sign of love and a promise to marry.

Pinecones are often added to wreaths, to represent hope, promise and renewal. The Christmas rose, though not evergreen, does blossom in the cold snows of winter and has been an enduring symbol of love and generosity. During the Victorian Era, many plants carried a specific message that people recognized instantly. Creating a wreath using such plants sent a clear message of everlasting love, peace and prosperity.

Bibliography

Barrow, Mary. "Father Christmas." www.woodlands-junior.kent.sch.uk , viewed 2013.

Bergman, Kalle. "Saint Lucia Dan and Swedish Lussebullar." www.huggingtonpost.com, published 2010, viewed 2013.

Bowler, Gerry. *The World Encyclopedia of Christmas*. McClelland and Stewart Ltd., Canada, 2000.

Calandra, John D. "The Legend of La Befana." Italian American Institute 1997-2000, www.qcpaes.qc.edu, viewed 2013.

Christmas Around the World, New Orchard Editions Ltd., Robert Rogers House, Dorset England, Blandford Press Ltd. 1978.

Del Re, Gerard and Patricia. *The Christmas Almanack*. Doubleday and Co., New York, 1979.

DeWinter, Haarlem. "Santa Claus's Dutch Uncle." www.wsj.com, viewed 2013.

DiMeglio, Francesca. "I'm a Believer Stories of the Italian Christmas Witch." www.italiansrus.com, viewed 2013.

Drum, Walter. "Magi in The Catholic Encyclopedia." Robert Appleton Co. www.newadvent.org, published 1910, 2012, viewed 2013.

Gordon, John Steel. "A Brief History of Christmas." www.wsj.com, published 2007, viewed 2013.

Gould, S.J. "The Case of the Irish Elk." www.ucmp.berkeley.edu, published 1977, viewed 2013.

Green, Thomas. "The History of Santa Claus and Father Christmas." www.arthuriana.co.uk, published 2004, 2012, viewed 2013.

Greenstone, Robyn. "Cloisters Museum Gallery Talk, The Image of the Rose." www.columbia.edu, published 1997, the Augustine Club, Columbia University, viewed 2013.

Haggerty, Bridget. "Irish Superstitions for the Christmas Season." www.irishcultureandcustoms.com, viewed 2013.

Haugan, Randolph. *Christmas - An American Annual of Christmas Literature and Art*. Augsburg Publishing House, Minneapolis. Volumes 20-22, 1950-1952.

Heij, Anja. "How Odin Became Santa Claus: Symbolism and Pagan Origins of a Gift-Giver Saint." www.realmagick.com, viewed 2013.

Hildesheim, John. Modernized by Morris, H.S. "The Three Kings of Cologne - A Legend of the Middle Ages." www.kraftmstr.com, viewed 2013.

Hill, Suzanne. "Flower Symbols in Christian Art." www.suite101.com, published 2007, viewed 2013.

Hubert von Staufer, Countess Maria. "The Christmas Archives. Customs from England." www.christmasarchives.com, viewed 2013.

Johnson, Bettye. "The Symbol of the Rose." www.authorsden.com, viewed 2013.

Lagerlof, Selma. "The Legend of the Christmas Rose." www.enotes.com, viewed 2013.

Lawless, Laura. "Christmas in France." www.about.com, viewed 2013.

Lewicki, James and Lillian. *The Golden Book of Christmas Tales - Legend from Many Lands*. Simon and Schuster, New York, 1956.

Haugan, Randolph. *Christmas - An American Annual of Christmas Literature and Art*. Augsburg Publishing House, Minneapolis. Volumes 20-22, 1950-1952.

McLean, Juelie. "Gift Givers of the World," "Everything You Wanted to Know About Saint Nicholas," www.santalady.com, published 1996-2005, viewed 2013.

Neale, John Mason. *Christmas Around the World*. 1853.

Pease, Glenn. "Christmas Animals based on Luke 2:1-20." www.sermoncentral.com, viewed 2013.

Picariello, Gary. "LaBefana - Italy's Good Witch Rules." www.voices.yahoo.com, viewed 2013.

Steedman, Amy. "Legends of Stories of Italy." www.mainlesson.com, viewed 2013.

Tarrant, Margaret and Heath, Marian Russell. *Christmas Garland*. Hale, Cushman and Flint Publishers, 1942.

The History of Santa - from 2000 BC to 20th Century. Duncan Royale. M.E. Duncan Co. CA ,1987.

Van de Meulen, Roel. "Sinterklass, A Dutch Tradition." www.galactic-guide.com, published 1994, 2010, viewed 2013.

Van Kampen, Henk. "Sinterklaas, the Number One Dutch Tradition." www.traceyourdutchroots.com, published Nov. 2008, viewed 2013.

Enjoy Your Own Gift Giver

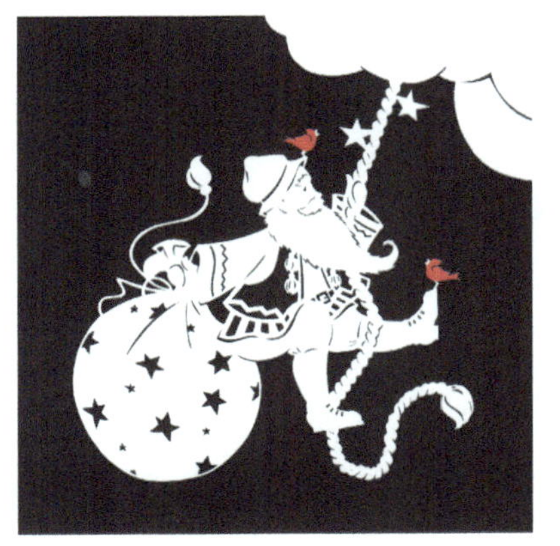 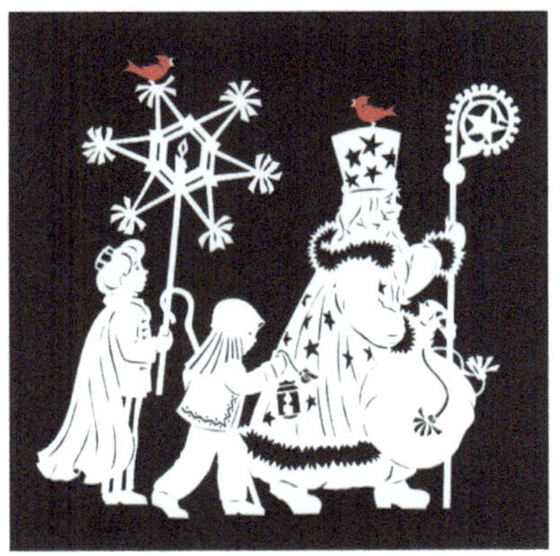 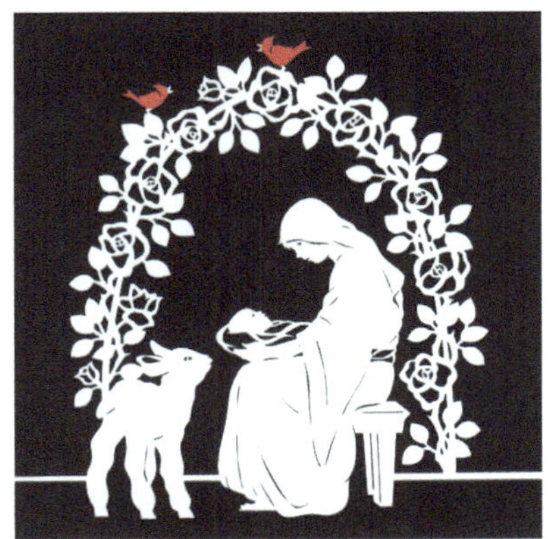

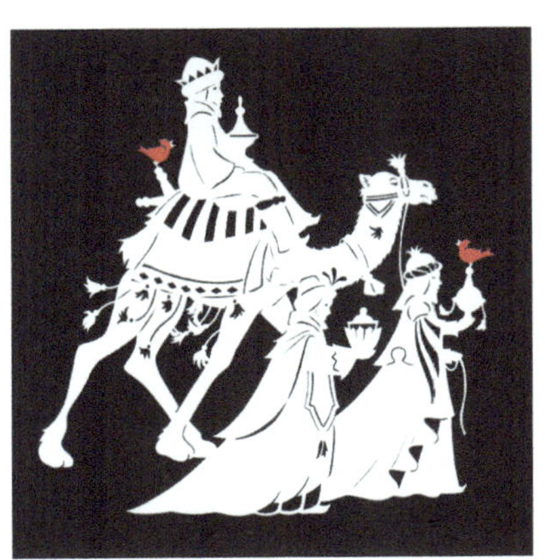 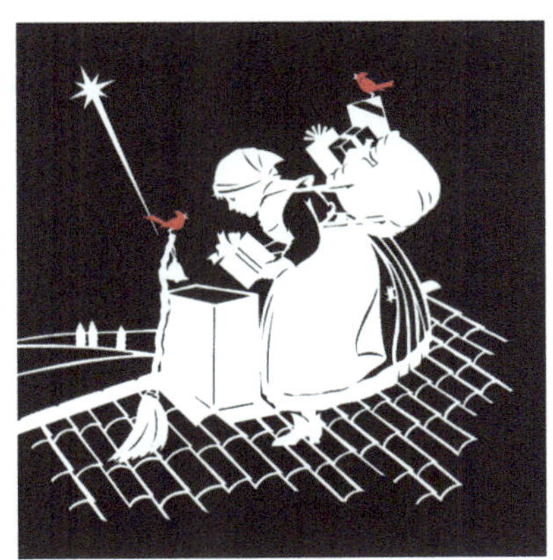 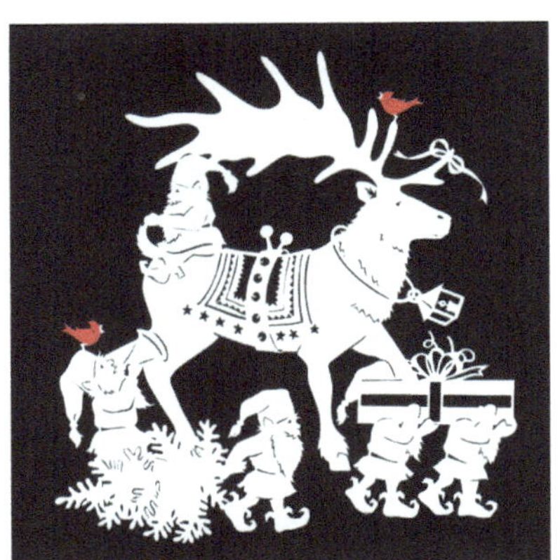

All of the gift giver papercuttings seen in *A Paper-Cut Christmas* can be purchased
as framed original artwork or prints online and at the Martha Link Walsh Gallery.

188 North Main Street, Route 1
Branford, Connecticut 06405
(203) 481-3505
www.marthalinkwalsh.com

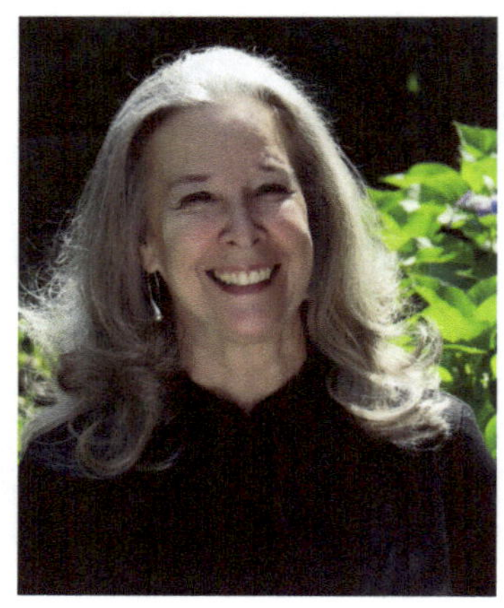

About the Artist

Martha Link Walsh has dared to devote her life to the art that she loves, and to serving the small community of Branford, Connecticut, where she has her studio and store, the Martha Link Walsh Gallery, www.marthalinkwalsh.com.

In a serendipitous interlude some 40 years ago, Ms. Walsh discovered the art of paper-cutting. From that point on, she has filled her days learning about the history of cut-paper styles and traditions and teaching herself to draw and cut. In the process, she has developed her own signature style, creating one-of-a-kind originals that touch the heart.

The essence of her art is about telling stories. Whether it is commemorating a personal milestone, a family's history, or holiday traditions, her paper-cuts illuminate and celebrate the occasion.

Her work has been featured in many publications, including *Colonial Homes, Victoria, Early American Life,* and *Humane Education.*